Hot Damn & Hell Yeah: Recipes for Hungry Banditos & The Dirty South
by Ryan Splint and Vanessa Johnson

This is Microcosm #76030

ISBN #978-0-9770557-0-8

First Edition, 3,000 copies, October 1, 2005
Second Edition, 3,000 copies - March 1, 2007
Third Edition, 5,000 copies - November 1, 2008

Cover design by Sparky Taylor
Back cover and spine by Joe Biel
Cover illustrations by Ryan Splint & Sarah Oleksyk.

Hot Damn & Hell Yeah illustrations, layout, and recipes by Ryan Splint

The Dirty South Recipes by Vanessa Johnson. Typed by Webly Bowles. Edited by Brittney Willis, Joe Biel and Zach Evans. Illustrations by Sarah Oleksyk. Titles by Alex Wrekk. Layout by Joe Biel.

Printed in Canada by Lebonfon

Microcosm Publishing
222 S Rogers St.
Bloomington, IN 47404
(812)323-7395
Other zines, books, stickers, patches, pins, posters, t-shirts, DVDs, & more:
www.microcosmpublishing.com

Howdy y'all

This chunk a' paper yer holdin' amounts to a helluva lot of cookin' over a number of years on my part. Having a fair amount of experience in the kitchen under my belt didn't amount to much when I set out to avoid cookin' critters as part of my meals. As any folk who've tried this will tell you, there's a whole lotta bad vegetable-only food out there. There's also a lotta people that think pompous attitudes and morality lectures oughta be served alongside with it, maybe ta make up for the lack of flavor in their food. It ain't too hard to see why vegetarian food and the people who eat it haven't wound up with the best of reputations.

But don't let that fool ya or put a scare into ya about what's comin' up.

This ain't about who's got a right to eat what, or what should and shouldn't be on yer plate for proper eatin'. Hell, it ain't even about *healthy* eating –recipes like Bourbon Whiskey BBQ Sauce (p.11), Country-Fried Tofu (p.38) or just the size of the Dessert chapter (p.46) oughta convince ya of that much.

What it's about is food without obscure ingredients, that's easy to make and don't taste like sawdust even though it ain't chock-full a' butter, grease and meat. I've had to wade through my share of bland and downright horrible food in order to learn how ta get by cooking without meat or dairy. Now I ain't no master chef, but I figure I've done a decent job of it and wound up with some good recipes. Be a damn shame if I never got a chance to pass what ah've learned on ta other folks, so I've collected some of the best recipes I got from various people and places, and finally wrote down others I've been making from scratch as situations have called for 'em. Now they're all yers fer the takin' and should work well for ya (maybe better if read usin' yer best southern accent, but no guarantees on that).

Just before we hit the trail, I'd like to thank all the folks who've passed on recipes to me over the years, cooked for me, or been brave enough to let me cook for them - my apologies to some of y'all out there who fit inta that last category.

Thanks most of all to mah numero uno cookin' compañero, who made me a cookbook all mah own to write in, gettin' me started well on the way to doin' this. Muchas gracias, Senorita.

Alright folks, saddle up and let's get goin'….

–RYAN

hotdamn_cookzine@yahoo.com.au

TABLE OF CONTENTS

DESERTS

A FEW TIPS FOR YA

...ABOUT INGREDIENTS

One a' the hardest things I found when learnin' to cook food without meat or dairy was understandin' what half the ingredients in a lot of vegetarian recipes were, let alone where ya might find 'em. Ah s'pose sometimes people deadset on makin' food that's healthy plumb fergit that the rest of us gotta be able to decipher what they're puttin' in it. Last thing ya wanna do is travel to the ends a' the earth lookin' fer powdered root of something-or-other to complete yer dinner. Fer both yer sanity and mine, I stick to usin' simpler ingredients in my recipes, but some are still less commonly known or may be completely new to ya, so here they are:

TVP (TEXTURED VEGETABLE PROTEIN)

TVP is made from soy beans and usually sold as dehydrated granules – if mixed with hot water, it rehydrates and takes on the texture of minced beef. When used in yer cookin', I think you'll find it rare people will notice it ain't the real thing. Ya shouldn't have too much trouble trackin' this down in the health food section of yer grocery store or nearly any whole foods store.

NUTRITIONAL YEAST

This is a yellow-brown, nearly powdered substance that usually shows up in recipes where yer after a cheesy flavor of some sort. Ya kin usually track this down at health food or whole food stores, but ah'll admit sometimes ya have a helluva time findin' it. Some folks might try sellin' you Brewer's Yeast instead, but don't fall fer that – it ain't even close to the same thing. Unfortunately, there's no decent substitute for Nutritional Yeast, so good luck huntin' it down.

SOY MILK

Soy milk is basically the liquid leftover from boiling soybeans, and is used in place of dairy-based milk in recipes. Like other milks, it also curdles when mixed with a bit a' lemon juice so it's a great buttermilk substitute fer cookin' as well. Ya oughta have no trouble finding it in yer grocery store, as it's popular among the lactose-intolerant crowd. It's also usually fortified with extra vitamins so yer gettin' a bit of a nutritional bonus without havin' to lift a finger. I usually opt fer the vanilla-flavored type since it doesn't taste as chalky as the plain variety.

TOFU

Tofu is pressed soybean curd, and used as an alternative ta meat and dairy. It's sold packed in water, so you'll need to squeeze and drain it ta get the best results (see below). There are two main types you'll find poppin' up in here:

- FIRM TOFU -

Yep, this is a firm block of tofu, usually used instead a' beef or chicken in food. It's got a texture like a spongy cheese, and like a sponge you'll need to squeeze it out so it'll absorb flavor better when cookin' or marinatin'. Just take yer block of tofu out've the package and shake it off over the sink, ta start with. Then, cut it into slices and lay them in a single layer on a clean dishtowel. Wrap the dishtowel (or two) around yer sliced tofu, lay it on the kitchen bench, place a heavy object on top (preferably a flat one, ta press it evenly) and leave it that way fer 30 min. to an hour. When ya return, the dishtowels should have soaked up most of the water and the tofu should feel a whole lot drier. Now it'll soak up flavor better when you cook or marinate it as a substitute fer beef or chicken in yer cookin'

☠For a "meatier" texture, remove firm tofu from its packaging and drain the excess liquid, then freeze it in an airtight container. Once thawed, the firm tofu will be much chewier/rigid and can be squeezed and marinated as per usual.

- SILKEN TOFU -

Silken tofu is also made of pressed soybean curd, but the texture is completely different than firm tofu. It's useful in dips or as an egg substitute in pies or bread, but it also contains a lot more water that ya need to get rid of before using it. Otherwise, it'll turn whatever yer makin' into a soupy mess. Unfortunately, ya can't just squeeze it like ya do firm tofu – it'll just crumble inta watery slop if ya try. The best way I've come across to get water outta silken tofu is with cheesecloth. It may take a bit of time, but believe me pardner: it's better than spending the time to make food only ta have it ruined by too much moisture.

Get some cheesecloth from yer local grocery and place the silken tofu in the center of a square made from a few layers a' that. Pull the corners together and hold it by them as ya pick it up so the tofu is suspended in the center of the cheesecloth. Hold it over the sink and slowly twist the tofu in one direction, making the cheesecloth tighten around it. Water will start seepin' through the cheesecloth – wipe it off so it drips inta the sink and keep slowly twisting, wiping off the water as it comes out. Be patient and careful not to squeeze too hard, or you'll start squeezin' out tofu, too. Check how watery the tofu is, and continue gently squeezing the water out until it's considerably drier than what ya started with. It oughta resemble cottage cheese more than white jelly when yer done.

...ABOUT SUBSTITUTIONS

I feel ah've gotta at least warn ya about substitutin' ingredients in recipes. Like I said earlier, I aim ta make my food with basic ingredients and I have total confidence in 'em that way. I've seen some a' the simplest and tastiest recipes shot all ta hell 'cause someone tried substitutin' ingredients without understandin' what it'd do to the taste. Can't say I haven't made the same mistake myself, either. I encourage experimentin' with food – that's how most recipes here came about – but if yer itchin' to try doin' it with these recipes, keep that finger pointed squarely at yerself ta blame if ya wind up with a mouthful tastin' worse than dirt. I guarantee all these recipes ta taste great, but if ya deviate from what's written you take responsibility for the results, fer better or worse.

CAROB VERSUS COCOA

Now I don't rightly know who started the idea of carob being a fine substitute fer cocoa, but those folks've got a lot ta answer for. I know I ain't the only one who's been suckered in by the promise of a tasty alternative to chocolate, only to be sorely disappointed and lookin' fer a rubbish bin. Carob ain't in the same league as cocoa; hell, it comes from a completely different plant, so danged if I know what possessed folk to bill it as a good substitute. Ya won't find carob being used in any of the recipes here, and I discourage usin' it thinkin' you'll get a flavor tasting anywhere near as good. Carob is used in dog treats, and I don't know about y'all, but I've seen dogs eat some downright disturbin' things . . . keep that in mind next time yer considerin' the merits of carob versus cocoa in yer cookin'

CANNED, FROZEN OR FRESH VEGETABLES

Some of the recipes here, especially the soups and chilis, call fer vegetables ya kin buy fresh, frozen or canned. Ya kin use any of them in yer recipes and the canned and frozen variety'll save ya time and worryin' about spoiled vegetables (one normal can of vegetables is equal to about 1 ½ C.). Just keep in mind how it'll affect yer cooking times and taste. Fresh vegetables will need to be cooked ta get 'em out of a raw state, but they'll have the best flavor and texture out've the three. Frozen vegetables will need to thaw and reheat while cooking, but they're almost as good as fresh vegetables for taste and texture. Canned vegetables are already cooked, but are usually packed in salt water and sometimes can take on the taste of the can because of it. What ya make up for in time with canned vegetables, ya tend ta lose in the taste and texture. In the end, no matter what ya use you'll still get a hearty meal and a full stomach so don't dwell on it much.

MEAT AND DAIRY

Luckily, food without meat and dairy ain't all salads, bread and water like most folks think. Figurin' out what to substitute for meat and dairy in food was the hardest part of adjusting to cookin' this way. Here's how I sorted it all out for the recipes you'll find in here, in case ya wanna try convertin' recipes of yer own or switch some a' these to a meat and dairy variety:

THIS:	IS SUBSTITUTED WITH:
Beef	Firm Tofu marinated beef-style _or_ TVP granules (instead of minced beef)
Chicken	Firm Tofu marinated chicken-style
Milk	Soy Milk
Buttermilk (about 1 C.)	1 C. Soy Milk mixed with 1 T. lemon juice
Sweetened Condensed Milk (about 1 C.)	2 C. Soy Milk reduced to 1 C. and mixed with 1 C. powdered sugar
Egg (1)	Egg replacer powder (per directions) _or_ ¼ C. silken tofu, squeezed and drained _or_ 1 tsp. baking powder + ½ tsp. baking soda + 2 T. flour + 3 T. water, mixed well

SAUCES AND MIXES

WORCHESTERSHIRE SAUCE

Easy Worcestershire sauce ya kin make on yer own, without them pesky anchovies in it

1 C. cider vinegar
1/3 C. dark molasses
¼ C. soy sauce
¼ C. water
3 T. lemon juice
1½ tsp. salt
1½ tsp. mustard powder
1 tsp onion powder
¾ tsp. ground ginger
½ tsp. black pepper
¼ tsp. garlic granules
¼ tsp. cayenne pepper

Mix ingredients well in a saucepan and boil a minute or so. Let the sauce cool and then transfer into a container to store in refrigerator. Shake well before usin'

CHEESE SAUCE

Dairy-free cheese-flavor sauce ta use on pasta, vegetables, Nachos (p.34), Enchiladas (p.35) or whatever else ya think of. Add extra ingredients ta modify the flavor a bit

1/3 C. nutritional yeast
½ C. flour
1 T. dried onion
1/8 tsp. turmeric
1/8 tsp. pepper
6 T. olive oil
2 tsp. prepared (bottled) mustard
2 tsp. salt
½ C. ketchup
1¾ C. water

Blend all ingredients well in a saucepan over medium heat, whisking continuously until it comes to a boil and thickens to yer liking. It'll continue ta thicken as it cools, so it's best hot. To reheat, add a bit of water and stir well over low heat

MUSHROOM GRAVY

A great all-purpose gravy ya kin use for mashed potatoes, Pot Pies (p.42), or wherever else a meal cries out in the night fer some gravy

2 C. water
2 T. vegetable oil
3 T. nutritional yeast
1 tsp. vegetable stock powder
½ C. fresh mushrooms, diced
½ C. onion, finely chopped
½ tsp. onion salt
flour

Mix all ingredients except flour in a saucepan and heat to a simmer. Slowly add flour a Tablespoon at a time and whisk well after each addition, until gravy thickens up to yer liking. Try addin' some fresh-cracked black pepper in, too

EASY GRAVY

A simple, fast-food style gravy. Try it on Country-Style Biscuits (p. 16), put it ta use on a Vegetable Mountain (p.41), hot chips or anything else ya might wanna slather in gravy

2 T. oil
4 T. flour
3 C. broth of desired gravy flavor
¼-½ tsp. salt (to taste)
¼ tsp. pepper
¼ tsp. sugar

Heat oil in a saucepan over medium heat and sprinkle in flour, stirring well to remove clumps. Continue heating mixture, stirring often until it turns a darker brown, 5-10 minutes. Add remaining ingredients, stir well and bring to a boil. Reduce heat and simmer until gravy reduces and thickens ta how ya like it

BEEF-STYLE MARINADE

Fer adding beef flavor ta yer firm tofu – mix it all together and marinate away

¼ C. soy sauce
½ C. water
1½ tsp. garlic powder
1½ tsp. ground ginger
1 tsp. fresh ground black pepper
1 tsp. beef or vegetable broth powder (optional)

CHICKEN-STYLE MARINADE

Fer adding a chicken flavor ta yer firm tofu – mix well and marinate at will

2 ½ T. chicken-style broth powder
1 tsp. rice vinegar
2 T. soy sauce
½ C. boiling water
2 T. BBQ sauce (p. 11)
fresh ground pepper (to taste)
1/8 tsp. each of:
- paprika
- rosemary
- garlic powder
- onion powder
- basil
- parsley
- oregano

MEXICAN CHILI GRAVY

This is called for if ya make Enchiladas (p. 35), but it's a good topping any ol' time

1 T. vegetable oil
½ C. onion, chopped
1-3 tsp. chili powder (to taste)
1/8 tsp. salt
1 T. flour
¼ tsp. garlic powder
½ tsp. cumin
3 T. tomato paste
1/8 tsp. cayenne pepper
1 C. chicken-flavored broth

Heat oil in a small saucepan over medium heat and cook onion 'til translucent. Mix spices and flour together and stir in well with the onion, making sure there's no lumps. Mix tomato paste and water together and pour it inta the saucepan. Mix well and boil fer a few minutes, stirring to prevent clumps or scorching Stir in extra flour to thicken more, or add extra spices to suit yer taste

SALSA

Once ya make a batch u' this, you'll wonder why ya usually buy the stuff

1 can chopped tomatoes
1 ½ C. water
½ C. green bell pepper, chopped
½ C. red bell pepper, chopped
1 small Spanish onion, chopped
1 stalk celery, finely chopped
1/3 C. tomato paste
¼ tsp. salt
2 T. white vinegar
¼ tsp. dried garlic granules
¼ C. jalapeno peppers, chopped – this'll make yer salsa MEDIUM HOT
    - 2 T. jalapenos is MILD   - 1/3 C. jalapenos is HOT

Combine all ingredients in a saucepan over medium heat. Bring to a boil then reduce heat and simmer for 30 minutes or until thickened. Cool, transfer to a container and refrigerate it overnight to let the flavors combine before usin'

BLACK BEAN SALSA

*A different style a' salsa, more fer as a dip with tortilla chips rather than accompanyin'
meals. Once ya taste it though, ya might have trouble decidin' which ya prefer*

3 C. black beans, cooked and drained
1 C. corn kernels, cooked and drained
1 Spanish onion, chopped
3 tomatoes, seeded and chopped
1 C. green onions, chopped
1 red bell pepper, chopped (optional)
1 T. white vinegar
3 T. lime juice
1/2 tsp. black pepper
1 tsp. cumin
1 C. cilantro, chopped
1/2 tsp. salt

Combine all ingredients in a large container and toss well. Refrigerate overnight
to allow flavors to blend, tossing well again before serving cold

GUACAMOLE

*Ah, good ol' Guacamole . . . this'll pop up as a topping for Enchiladas (p.35) and Nachos
(p.34), but just whip it up to dip some tortilla chips in and you'll love it just as much*

2 ripe avocados, cut in half and pitted
1 clove garlic, crushed
1 tsp. lemon juice
½ tsp. salt
¼ tsp. black pepper
1/8 tsp. cayenne pepper
1 T. olive oil (optional)
½ C. green onions, chopped (optional)
1 fresh tomato, chopped (optional)

Remove avocado from skins and mash with a fork in a medium-size bowl. Add
remaining ingredients and mix well. Refrigerate covered until yer ready to use it

SOUTHERN-FRIED SPICE MIX

A mix of spices to use for Country-Fried Tofu (p.38) or whatever else yer lookin' to fry up

2 C. flour
½ tsp. each of:
- salt
- thyme
- dried basil
- dried oregano
1 T. each of:
- celery salt
- black pepper
- dry mustard
4 T. paprika
2 tsp. garlic salt
1 tsp. ground ginger
2 T. sugar

Mix all ingredients together in a large, sealable container ta store in 'til it's needed

ALMOST SOUR CREAM

This won't fool ya next ta the real thing, but it works well alongside other toppings like Guacamole (p.9) and Salsa (p.8) for Nachos (p.34) or Enchiladas (p.35)

1 ½ C. firm silken tofu, squeezed and drained
1 T. canola oil
2 tsp. lemon juice
2 tsp. cider vinegar
1 tsp. sugar
½ tsp. salt

Combine all the ingredients in a food processor or blender. Blend for several minutes to thicken it up. Refrigerate in an airtight container fer up to a week

SOY MAYONNAISE

This'll easily match or beat the taste of any soy mayonnaise ya find at the store

1 package silken tofu, firm or extra firm
1 T. cider vinegar
1 T. lemon juice
1 T. sugar
1 T. Dijon mustard
½ tsp. salt
1/3 - ½ C. oil

Place all ingredients except oil in a food processor or blender and puree on high speed a few minutes, until smooth. Add oil 1 T. at a time, and puree a few more minutes after each addition until ya got a thicker, creamy texture

BOURBON WHISKEY BBQ SAUCE

Ya might be lookin' ta just drink this, but it's actually a mighty fine BBQ sauce too

¼ C. Worcestershire sauce (p. 5)
¼ C. onion, minced
4 cloves garlic, minced
¾ C. bourbon whiskey
2 C. ketchup
¼ C. tomato paste
1/3 C. apple cider vinegar
½ tsp. Tabasco sauce
½ C. brown sugar
½ tsp. black pepper
1½ tsp. salt

Sauté onion and garlic with the bourbon in a skillet over medium heat, until onion is translucent. Add remaining ingredients, mix well and bring to a boil. Reduce heat and simmer for 20 minutes, stirring occasionally. Strain or puree it if ya want a smoother consistency. Store refrigerated in an airtight container

BREADS

FLOUR TORTILLAS

These are downright essential fer Burritos (p.31 and 32), Fajitas (p.34), and even some desserts (p.58). This'll make 5-10 tortillas, depending on how large ya make 'em

2 ½ C. flour
1 tsp. salt
¼ C. margarine or oil
¾ C. boiling water

Stir flour and salt together in a large bowl. Rub the margarine in by hand until evenly mixed, then hollow out a well in the center of yer ingredients and pour the boiling water into it. Mix with a fork or wooden spoon until you've got a doughy texture to work with

Sprinkle a bit of flour on top and knead the dough until it's a smooth consistency without sticking ta yer fingers

Roll pieces of dough into balls about 5cm/2-inches around, then place on a tray and cover 'em. Leave covered an hour or more before movin' on

Roll the dough balls out on a lightly floured surface to the thickness yer after, then get a skillet or griddle warmed up over high heat

Place a tortilla on your cooking surface for about 10 seconds. Flip over as soon as you see a bubble or two formin' on top

Cook 20 – 30 seconds then flip back over to cook the other side 15-20 more seconds, and keep a close eye on 'em – yer after tortillas cooked but soft with light brown spots, not crispy with dark brown spots

Stack cooked tortillas on a plate covered with a dish towel to keep soft until yer ready for 'em. They can be refrigerated and reheated fer later use as well

CORN TORTILLAS

Now you may not find these as tasty or as commonly used as the flour variety, but this recipe'll make 6 corn tortillas that you'll need to make enchiladas (p.35) for yer gang

¾ **C. cornmeal**
¾ **C. flour**
¼ **tsp. salt**
1 **tsp. baking powder**
½ **C. boiling water**

Stir dry ingredients together in a large bowl until well mixed.

Stir in the boiling water to form a brittle dough, then knead with your hands until the dough holds together well and you get a smoother consistency. It might still feel a bit gritty, but that'll just be from the cornmeal so don't worry none

Divide and roll the dough inta six balls, then place them on a tray and cover fer about 30 minutes. This'll make 'em easier for ya to roll out

Flatten each ball with yer hand, then roll 'em out on a lightly floured surface

Heat a lightly oiled skillet over medium heat and cook each tortilla until light brown on each side. A trick ta doin' this is only cooking 20 seconds at a time on each side, constantly flipping 'em over until they're evenly cooked

Keep cooked tortillas on a covered plate until you're ready to use 'em.

CORNBREAD

Cornbread is a must-have when eatin' Chilis (p 26-28) or some cajun food (p.20), but try it with a bit of honey or jam for a treat, it's that good on its own

2/3 C. white sugar
2 C. flour
1 tsp. salt
1 T. baking powder
1/3 C. margarine, softened
¾ C. cornmeal
1 tsp. vanilla extract
1 1/3 C. soy milk
2 egg substitutes
Dash of cayenne pepper (optional)

Preheat oven to 200° C/400° F and coat a 20cm/8-inch baking pan lightly with cooking spray or margarine

Beat sugar, salt, margarine, and vanilla together in a large bowl until creamy
Stir in yer egg substitutes one at a time, mixing well after each

In a smaller bowl, mix flour, baking powder, cornmeal and cayenne pepper together

Alternate stirring the flour mixture and soy milk into the sugar mixture, beating well after each addition

Pour batter into greased pan and bake in preheated oven for 20-25 minutes, until golden brown and a toothpick or knife inserted into center comes out clean

HUSH PUPPIES

These li'l Cajun-style breads suit Red Beans and Rice (p.20) or Chilis (p.26-28) nicely

1 C. cornmeal
½ tsp. salt
½ C. flour
½ tsp. baking powder
2 egg substitutes
¼ tsp. baking soda
½ C. soymilk mixed with
      2 tsp. lemon juice
¼ C. parsley, finely chopped
1 T. vegetable oil
½ C. green onions, finely chopped
½ tsp. cayenne pepper
¼ tsp. garlic powder
1/8 tsp. black pepper
1/8 tsp. chili powder

In a large bowl, combine all dry ingredients and blend well. Add the remaining ingredients one at a time, mixing well after each addition

Form the mixture into spoon-sized balls and deep fry in oil until golden brown, or ya don't have a fryer, make into patties and fry in a skillet coated well with oil

COUNTRY-STYLE BISCUITS

These quick and easy "buttermilk" flavor Biscuits can be used in Biscuits and Gravy (p. 38) for breakfast or topped with Easy Gravy (p. 6) for some noon/ night-time eatin'

2 C. flour
1 T. baking powder
1 tsp. salt
3 T. margarine
2/3 C. soy milk mixed with
    2 tsp. lemon juice

Preheat oven to 200° C/400° F and lightly grease a baking tray

Combine flour, baking powder and salt together in a medium-sized bowl

Cut margarine into flour mixture until you've got a crumbly mixture ta work with

Gradually stir in enough of the soy milk mixture until a dough is formed that is moist but not sticky – it should hold together enough for you to knead it, but not stick to yer fingers or the bowl it's in

Remove dough from bowl and knead a few times on a lightly floured surface. Roll out to a 2 cm/¾-inch thickness and cut into circles using an overturned drinking glass or other cutter

Bake in preheated oven for 10-15 minutes until lightly browned. Serve pipin' hot

PANCAKES

Serve these up any ol' time of the day, but fergit that "syrup-flavored" topping - go the extra mile with 100% Maple Syrup ta have 'em taste best!

1 C. flour
½ tsp. salt
2 ½ tsp. baking powder
2 T. sugar
dash of nutmeg
2 egg substitutes
2 T. margarine, melted
½ tsp. vanilla extract
1 C. soymilk mixed with
      1 T. lemon juice

Sift all the dry ingredients together in a medium-sized bowl. In separate bowl, mix the wet ingredients together

Stir your wet ingredients into the dry ingredients just until they're blended – overmixin' won't get you anything but tough pancakes, pardner

Grease a skillet or griddle with non-stick cooking spray or margarine and place over medium heat

Pour batter into skillet 1/3 C. at a time and cook until lightly browned on the bottom, then flip with a thin spatula and cook the other side. Serve warm

CRANBERRY SCONES

These are good eatin' for lazy mornings at the bandito hideout

2 C. flour
3 tsp. baking powder
½ tsp. baking soda
2 T. white sugar
¼ tsp. salt
1 tsp. grated lemon rind
½ C. margarine
½ C. dried cranberries
2/3 C. soy milk mixed with
    2 tsp. lemon juice

Preheat oven to 220° C/425° F

Combine first six ingredients in a large bowl and cut in margarine with pastry blender or two knives, until mixture is crumbly.

Add dried cranberries to the bowl and toss lightly to coat 'em with the mix

Add soy milk mixture and stir until dry ingredients are moistened to form dough

Turn out dough onto lightly floured surface and knead five or six times

Divide dough in half and shape each half into a ball. Flatten both balls into 18 cm/7 inch circles on an ungreased baking sheet

Use a knife to cut three deep lines in each to create six wedges of dough, but don't separate them – these'll break right off nicely once they're properly baked

Bake in preheated oven for 10-15 minutes, until lightly browned. Transfer as a whole to wire racks to cool slightly, *then* break 'em into wedges

PUMPKIN BREAD

Eat this warm on a cold day and yer liable ta wanna eat it all at once

2 C. pumpkin, cooked and pureed
¼ C. oil or applesauce
2 egg substitutes
1 C. white sugar
2 C. flour
2 tsp. baking powder
1 tsp. baking soda
½ tsp. ground cinnamon
½ tsp. ground nutmeg
¼ tsp. ground cloves
¼ tsp. ground ginger
½ C. raisins
½ C. walnuts, chopped

Preheat oven to 175° C/350° F. Spray a loaf pan with non-stick cooking spray and a dust lightly with flour

Mix pumpkin, oil/applesauce, egg substitutes and sugar together in a large bowl. In a separate bowl, mix together the flour, baking powder, baking soda and spices. Stir the flour mixture into the pumpkin mixture until just blended   Stir in the raisins and walnuts until even distributed, then pour the batter into the prepared loaf pan and place in the center of the oven. Bake for 50 minutes or until a knife inserted into center of loaf comes out clean - it may take a bit longer

SIDE DISHES

REFRIED BEANS

You'll find these handy fer Nachos (p.34) and Enchiladas (p.35), just fer starters

3 C. beans (kidney, black or pinto), cooked and drained
1 ½ C. water
1 T. dried minced onion
½ tsp. salt

Combine all ingredients in a medium-sized saucepan and bring to a boil over medium heat. Lower heat and simmer about 10 minutes, until cooked beans soften. Mash beans and return to a simmer for another 10-20 minutes, until liquid reduces and beans thicken. Stir frequently to prevent scorchin' on bottom of pan

SPANISH RICE

Use this in yer Enchiladas (p.35) or just eaten next ta Fajitas (p. 34) or Burritos (p. 31-32)

1 C. rice, uncooked
1 onion, chopped
1 green bell pepper, chopped
2 T. vegetable oil
1 stalk celery, finely chopped
1 can chopped tomatoes
1 tsp. paprika
½ t. cumin
1/8 tsp. black pepper
1/8 tsp. salt
½ tsp. oregano
1/8 tsp cayenne pepper

Cook rice and set aside. Heat oil in a skillet over medium heat and sauté onion a few minutes until it becomes translucent. Add bell pepper, celery and spices, and cook fer another five minutes

Add chopped tomatoes and cooked rice – it oughta have a bit of a soupy consistency. Simmer until it reduces, stirring occasionally to ensure flavors mix and it ain't scorchin'. Add extra spices before servin' if it ain't quite ta yer taste

RED BEANS AND RICE

Some Cajun cookin' – good n' spicy. Try with Hush Puppies (p.15) or Cornbread (p.14)

2 C. kidney beans, cooked and drained
3 C. cooked white rice
½ tsp. minced garlic
2 tsp. minced onion
¼ C. celery, finely chopped
½ C. green bell pepper, chopped
½ tsp. cayenne pepper
1/8 tsp. dried marjoram
¼ tsp. paprika
1-2 T. chili powder (to taste)
1 tsp. Cajun seasoning
1/8 tsp. dried oregano
1 ½ T. beef broth powder
2 tsp. Worcestershire sauce (p. 5)
2 tsp. brown sugar
1 tsp. Tabasco sauce
1 bay leaf
1 can chopped tomatoes with juice

Mix everything together in a large pot, and add just enough water to reach the top of yer ingredients. Stir well so spices mix and broth powder and sugar dissolve

Bring to a boil over medium heat, stirring to keep from scorching. Reduce heat and simmer uncovered 30-45 minutes, still stirring to prevent scorchin' until the liquid reduces and contents thicken slightly. Remove the bay leaf before servin'

21

ROASTED GARLIC AND HERB COUSCOUS

It's quick n' easy and it tastes mighty fine – only use fresh garlic ta prevent oil splatterin'

1 ¼ C. vegetable broth
1 C. dry couscous
½ tsp. Salt
2 cloves fresh garlic, minced
2 T. olive oil
¼ tsp. Black pepper
½ tsp. each of:
  - thyme
  - dried basil
  - paprika

Bring vegetable broth to a boil, then add salt and couscous; remove from heat and leave covered for 10 minutes. Heat oil in a small saucepan over low heat and cook garlic just until it begins to brown. Add spices and stir, cooking another 30 seconds before removing from heat. Fluff the couscous with a fork, then mix the roasted garlic and herbs in and stir well to mix the flavors

POTATO SALAD

Great fer picnics or alongside Lentil Burgers (p. 29) and Country-Fried Tofu (p. 38)

4 C. potatoes, chopped, steamed and cooled
½ C. celery, chopped
1/3 C. pickles, chopped
¼ C. onion, finely chopped
¼ C. green onions, sliced
½ C. red bell pepper, chopped
2 T. parsley, finely chopped
½ C. soy mayonnaise (p. 11)
1-2 T. American mustard
½ tsp. pepper
1/4 tsp. salt

In a medium bowl, combine all ingredients except the potatoes and mix well. Then, add the potatoes and toss well to coat. Refrigerate before serving

SOUPS AND CHILIS

GARLIC SOUP

This'll cure what ails you! If it doesn't at least get yer nose running, well ah got some bad news - there's no hope for ya, pardner. This recipe makes a lot, so scale it down if ya gotta

1 large onion, chopped
2 bulbs of garlic cloves, separated and peeled
2 stalks celery, sliced
2 carrots, sliced
4 large potatoes, cubed
2 C. cabbage, chopped (optional)
1 C. frozen corn kernels (optional)
1 tsp. salt
1 tsp. cracked black pepper
½ tsp. cayenne pepper

Fill a large pot halfway with water and bring to a boil. Add the onion, garlic, celery and carrots. Cook 5-10 minutes then add yer remaining ingredients and return it all to a boil. Reduce heat and simmer for 20-30 more minutes, stirring occasionally. Purée cooked soup so it's only slightly chunky before serving

VEGETABLE SOUP

A chunky vegetable soup ta warm ya up on those cold days and nights

2 C. broth (chicken, beef or vegetable flavor)
2 cans diced tomatoes
1 onion, chopped
1 large potato, cubed
2 carrots, sliced
2 stalks celery, sliced
1 C. green beans
1 C. corn kernels
½ tsp. salt
½ tsp. garlic powder

Combine all ingredients in a large pot and bring to a boil. Reduce heat to simmer for 30 minutes, until vegetables are tender. Try adding fresh-cracked pepper

PUMPKIN SOUP

If ya got a bit of pumpkin on hand, try whippin' up this soup on a cold winter day

4 c. fresh pumpkin, chopped
1 C. cauliflower, chopped
1 red bell pepper, chopped
1 onion, chopped
2 T. vegetable oil
2 T. fresh ginger, chopped
2 tsp. chicken-flavor stock powder
1 ½ C. water
1 can coconut cream
1 tsp. chili pepper, chopped
1 T. lemon juice
1 T. tomato paste
1/8 tsp. sugar
¼ tsp. fresh cracked black pepper
Salt to taste
2 T. cilantro, chopped (garnish)

In a medium size pot, sauté pumpkin, bell pepper, onion and cauliflower in oil over medium heat for about five minutes. Add ginger, water and chicken stock powder. Bring to a boil, then reduce heat and simmer for 15 minutes

Add remaining ingredients except cilantro, and return to a boil for five minutes. Puree soup in a blender if ya like it smooth, and serve garnished with cilantro

VEGETABLE MINESTRONE

Why settle fer heatin' minestrone outta some can when ya kin make it better on yer own?

2 T. olive oil
1 onion, chopped
1 clove garlic, minced
1 C. celery, chopped
1 C. carrots, sliced
1 C. chicken flavored broth
3 C. water
1 C. tomato paste
1½ C. kidney beans, cooked and drained
1 C. green beans
2 C. spinach, chopped
1 C. zucchini, chopped
2 T. oregano
1 T. basil
½ tsp. salt
½ tsp. pepper
1 C. rollini pasta, uncooked

In a large pot, heat olive oil over medium heat. Sauté onion and garlic until onion becomes translucent. Add carrots and celery and sauté a few minutes more

Add broth, water, and tomato paste. Mix well and bring to a boil, stirring frequently. Add remaining ingredients except pasta and reduce heat to a simmer

Simmer fer 30-45 minutes, stirring occasionally. In a separate pot, cook the rollini pasta and drain. Stir cooked pasta inta hot soup just before serving

25

VEGETABLE CHILI

Dang near the best chili I've ever made - serve it up with Cornbread (p.14)

3 T. olive oil
1 medium onion, chopped
4 cloves garlic, minced
1 C. chopped mushrooms
2 C. chopped cauliflower pieces
3 C. corn kernels
1 large potato, peeled and cubed
2 carrots, chopped
1 green bell pepper, chopped
3 C. kidney beans, cooked and drained
1 can chopped tomatoes with juice
1 C. tomato juice or puree
2 T. chili powder
1 tsp. paprika
1 T. cumin
1/8 tsp. cayenne pepper
2 T. tomato paste
3 T. red wine vinegar

Heat oil in a large pot over medium heat. Sauté onions and garlic until onion is translucent, then add the mushrooms and sauté another 8-10 minutes

Stir in the rest of the ingredients one at a time and mix well after each addition

Bring the entire mixture to a boil, then reduce heat and simmer covered for about 30 minutes, stirring occasionally to prevent scorching on the bottom. Serve hot

26

BLACK BEAN CHILI

A different chili than the previous vegetable variety, but still good with Cornbread (p.14)

1 T. oil
1 onion, chopped
3 cloves garlic, minced
1 green bell pepper, chopped
3 C. black beans, cooked and drained
2 cans diced tomatoes
1 C. water
1-3 T. chili powder (to taste)
1 tsp. ground cumin
½ tsp. dried oregano
½ tsp. ground cinnamon
½ tsp. brown sugar
¼ tsp. salt
¼ tsp. black pepper
fresh cilantro or green onions, chopped (for garnish)

Heat oil in a large pot over medium heat. Add the onion, garlic and green bell pepper and sauté until onion is translucent. Stir in the chili powder, cumin, oregano and cinnamon, cooking until mixed and absorbed

Add the diced tomatoes and water, then bring to a boil, stirring occasionally to prevent burning to bottom of the pot. Add beans, sugar, salt and pepper. Stir well and return it to a boil. Reduce heat and simmer for 30 minutes, stirring to prevent any scorchin'. Serve garnished with cilantro or green onions

27

CHILI CON NON-CARNE

Another type a' chili – the original variety was just meat an' spices, but I wrangled it
'round ta accommodate mah slightly different tastes. Try it with some Cornbread (p.14)

1 C. TVP granules, dry
1 C. hot water
2 T. vegetable oil
1 onion, chopped
2 cloves garlic, chopped
2 cans chopped tomatoes
1 C. kidney beans, cooked and drained
½ tsp. salt
½ tsp. black pepper
3 tsp. ground cumin
1 tsp. chili powder
1 T. paprika
1 T. dried oregano
1 cinnamon stick
3 whole cloves

Combine TVP granules with hot water in a small bowl and set aside

Heat oil in a medium-sized pot over medium heat. Sauté the onion and garlic until
soft, then add the rehydrated TVP and tomatoes. Cover and allow to simmer 30
minutes, stirring occasionally. Stir in beans and cook until heated through

Remove whole cloves and the cinnamon stick before servin'

28

MAIN DISHES

LENTIL BURGERS

Lentil burgers are one of the easiest and tastiest bean burgers ya kin make. Have 'em on toasted buns with all the usual burger fixins, and see if ya don't go fer another

½ C. dry lentils
1 bay leaf
1 onion, finely diced
2 cloves garlic, crushed
1 T. olive oil
2 T. peanut butter
3 T. ketchup
½ tsp. thyme
1/8 tsp. black pepper
½ tsp. parsley
dash of salt
dash of Tabasco sauce (optional)
1 C. dry bread crumbs

Cover the lentils with water in a saucepan and simmer with the bay leaf for about 30 minutes. Once cooked, drain the lentils well and chuck out the bay leaf

Heat the olive oil in a saucepan or skillet over medium heat. Sauté the onion and garlic in the oil for a couple minutes, then place all yer ingredients except the breadcrumbs in a food processor or blender and blend for about 15 seconds

Pour contents in a large bowl and then stir in the bread crumbs – it'll still be pretty moist but should stick together all right. Form inta patties and cook in a lightly oiled skillet over medium heat until firm in center and slightly browned

BLACK BEAN BURGERS

Spicy bean burgers askin' to be topped with Salsa (p.8), Guacamole (p.9), Almost Sour Cream (p.10) and any other fixins ya like havin' on Tex-Mex food

½ C. rice, uncooked
3 C. black beans, cooked and drained
1 T. oil
1 small onion, chopped
½ red bell pepper, chopped
½ C. corn kernels
1 carrot, shredded
1 C. fresh tomato, seeded and chopped
¼ C. fresh cilantro, chopped (optional)
1 tsp. dried oregano
½ tsp. cumin
½ tsp. paprika
1 tsp. chili powder
1 tsp. garlic powder
¼ tsp. black pepper
1/8 tsp. salt
½ tsp. sugar
1 C. bread crumbs

Begin cookin' the rice while ya get down ta choppin' and sautéing the vegetables

Heat oil in a skillet over medium heat and sauté onion until translucent. Add bell pepper, tomato, cilantro and spices, sautéing five more minutes 'til tender

In a large bowl, combine sautéed vegetables with carrot, corn, beans and cooked rice. Mix and mash it well. Add ½ C. bread crumbs to the bowl and mix well with yer hands. Add more bread crumbs a bit at a time until it holds together well

Form the mix into patties and cook in a lightly oiled skillet over medium heat until patties are cooked and browned. Serve on toasted buns with toppings

BLACK BEAN AND SWEET POTATO BURRITOS

A different style a' burrito that's quick to make, mixin' sweet and spicy flavors topped with Salsa, Almost Sour Cream, green onions and cilantro to wrap it all up. Hot Damn!

Flour Tortillas (p. 12)
1 T. vegetable oil
½ C. onion, chopped
1 clove garlic, minced
3 T. chunky peanut butter
1 tsp. cumin
½ tsp. cinnamon
¼ tsp. cayenne pepper
3 C. sweet potatoes, cooked
1 C. black beans, cooked and drained
Salsa (p. 8)
Almost Sour Cream (p. 10)
¼ C. chopped green onions
2 T. chopped cilantro

Heat oil in a skillet over medium heat. Sauté the garlic and onion a few minutes until tender and onion is translucent

Stir in peanut butter, sweet potatoes and black beans, mashing slightly. Add in the spices and mix well, cooking a few more minutes until all the ingredients are heated through. Stir occasionally to prevent scorching

Serve in warm tortillas and top with salsa, sour cream, green onions and cilantro

BREAKFAST BURRITOS

Here's a hearty Southwestern breakfast for ya, with a bit of spice ta start yer day off

Flour Tortillas (p. 12)
2 T. oil
½ onion, chopped
1 clove garlic, minced
1 red bell pepper, sliced
1 C. mushrooms, sliced
1 C. corn kernels
1 carrot, peeled and chopped
1 potato, peeled and cubed
1 ½ C. black beans, cooked/drained
1 can diced tomatoes with juice
½ tsp. chili powder
1 tsp. cumin
2 T. brown sugar
½ tsp. turmeric
1/8 tsp. salt
2 T. flour

Heat oil in a large skillet over medium heat and sauté onion and garlic until tender. Add bell pepper and mushrooms and sauté a few minutes more before adding all remaining ingredients except fer the black beans

Stir well and heat through, then reduce heat and simmer for 10-15 minutes. Add black beans and sprinkle in flour, stirring well. Simmer another 10 minutes or until mixture thickens. Serve in warm tortillas and git yer day off to a good start

TACO AND BURRITO FILL
This is good in tortillas (p.12), but it's also used Nachos (p.34) and Enchiladas (p.35)

1 C. TVP granules, dry
2 C. boiling water
1 T. vegetable oil
1 onion, chopped
2 cloves garlic, minced
1 red bell pepper, chopped
1 can chopped tomatoes
1 tsp. paprika
2 tsp. chili powder
½ tsp. cumin
½ tsp garlic powder
1 T. Worcestershire sauce (p. 5, optional)
1/2 tsp. salt
1/8 tsp. black pepper
1/8 tsp. cayenne pepper
½ tsp. oregano (optional)

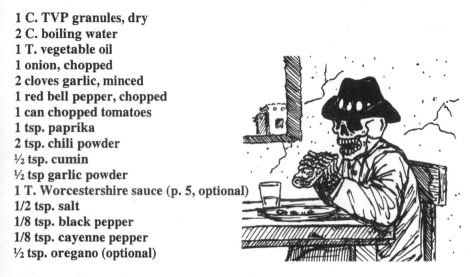

Combine TVP granules with 1 C. boiling water in a small bowl and set aside

In a skillet over medium-high heat, sauté onion and garlic in oil about five minutes, then add the bell pepper and sauté for another few minutes

Add the remaining ingredients, including rehydrated TVP granules. Add remaining 1 C. of water, mix well and bring it to a boil fer them flavors to mix

Reduce heat and simmer uncovered 20-30 minutes, stirring occasionally until the liquid reduces and it thickens. Serve in taco shells, tortillas or with tortilla chips

FAJITAS

Here's a simple Southwestern-style wrap ta fill ya up at the end of the day

Flour tortillas (p. 12)
1 package firm tofu, sliced in finger-size
    strips and marinated in chicken or beef-style marinade (p. 7)
2 T. oil
½ onion, sliced
1 red bell pepper, sliced into strips
1 garlic clove, minced
Guacamole (p. 9)
shredded lettuce
fresh tomatoes, chopped
fresh cilantro (optional)
fresh lime wedges or lime juice (optional)

Heat oil in a skillet over medium-high heat and sauté onion and garlic about five minutes, then add bell pepper and tofu strips. Cook until tofu strips are slightly browned and bell pepper is tender, stirring and tossing often to prevent burning. Serve on warm tortillas and topped with guacamole, lettuce and tomato. Top off with a dash of lime juice and some fresh cilantro if ya dare

NACHOS

Try this as just a layered dip fer the chips if ya prefer not havin' em go soggy while ya eat

1 bag tortilla chips
Refried beans (p. 20)
Taco and Burrito Fill (p. 33)
Cheese sauce (p. 5)
Guacamole (p. 9)
Almost Sour Cream (p. 10)
Salsa (p. 8)
½ C. tops of green onions (green stalks), chopped
½ C. fresh tomatoes, seeded and diced

Place some tortilla chips on a large plate, makin' a slight pit in the middle of 'em. Spoon refried beans into center. Cover refried beans with some of the cheese sauce. Spoon taco fill on top, then cover with remaining cheese sauce. Top with salsa, guacamole and sour cream, garnishing with green onions and tomatoes

ENCHILADAS

This is a good end-all, be-all meal fer packs a' hungry banditos and it ain't failed me yet

Corn Tortillas (p. 13)
Some or all of the following for filling:
    - Refried Beans (p. 20)
    - Spanish Rice (p. 20)
    - Taco and Burrito Fill (p. 33)
Cheese Sauce (p. 5)
Mexican Chili Gravy (p. 8)
Salsa (p. 8)
Guacamole (p. 9)
Almost Sour cream (p. 10)
Shredded lettuce
Chopped tomatoes
green onions, sliced

Preheat oven to 175° C/350° F and grease an 20 cm/8 in. square baking pan

Spoon yer preferred fillings and some cheese and/or chili sauce into the tortillas. Roll each filled tortilla and place in the baking dish with the seam facin' down

Once the baking dish is full, pour the remaining cheese and chili sauce overtop of the filled tortillas you've got packed together, spreading it around evenly to ensure all the tortillas are covered

Cover the whole thing in aluminium foil and bake in the preheated oven for 45 minutes. Serve topped with the salsa, guacamole and all the rest a' them fixins

COUSCOUS AND ROASTED VEGETABLES WITH DRESSING

This may be a bit involved, but it's a helluva dish that even tastes great cold

¼ C. + 2 T. olive oil
1 tsp. cumin
1½ tsp. rosemary, finely chopped
1 pkg. Frozen carrots and cauliflower
¼ tsp. black pepper
1 ½ C. vegetable broth
¾ C. couscous, uncooked
¼ tsp. crushed red pepper flakes
1 C. fresh tomatoes, seeded and diced
¼ C. orange juice
2 T. white wine vinegar
2 tsp. Dijon mustard
½ tsp. salt
1½ C. red kidney beans, cooked and drained
3 T. pine nuts
1/3 C. basil leaves, sliced into thin strips

Preheat oven to 200° C/400° F. Spray a baking pan with non-stick spray

In a large bowl, combine frozen vegetables with 1 tsp. of the rosemary and toss gently. Drizzle with 2T. olive oil, sprinkle with salt and pepper, and toss again to lightly coat. Spread vegetables in a single layer on the baking pan and place in oven for 12-15 minutes, until lightly browned and tender but crisp (they oughta be slightly soft but still snap if ya bend 'em)

While vegetables are cooking, get a small bowl and combine remaining olive oil and rosemary with the orange juice, cumin, Dijon mustard and vinegar. Blend well and set aside

In a medium saucepan, bring the broth to a boil. Remove from heat and stir in couscous and red pepper flakes. Cover and let stand 15 minutes

In a large bowl, combine roasted vegetables with basil strips, beans, tomatoes, and pine nuts. Toss lightly to mix. Fluff couscous with a fork and add to the bowl along with the dressing. Mix well and serve warm

SLOPPY JOES

Serve this pipin' hot on toasted buns and get yerself filled right up with a hearty meal

1 C. TVP granules, dry
2 T. vegetable oil
1 onion, diced
1 T. minced garlic
1 red bell pepper, diced
1 C. mushrooms, sliced
1 green bell pepper, diced
1 can diced tomatoes with juice
½ C. ketchup
2 T. Worcestershire sauce (p. 5)
1 T. tomato paste
¼ tsp. salt
½ tsp. black pepper
Hamburger buns, split and toasted

Combine TVP granules with 1 C. hot water in a bowl and set aside to soak

Heat oil in a skillet over medium heat and sauté the onion, bell pepper and garlic for about 5 minutes

Add mushrooms and cook for another few minutes before adding in yer remaining ingredients. Stir well and reduce heat, simmering for 10-20 minutes until it reduces and thickens a bit. Serve hot on toasted buns

THERE ARE TWO KINDS OF PEOPLE IN THE WORLD, MY FRIEND: THOSE WITH A NAPKIN AROUND THEIR NECK, AND THE PEOPLE WHO HAVE THE JOB OF DOING THE COOKING.

37

BISCUITS AND GRAVY

This'll sound downright strange to some folks, but give it a try I think you'll come around

Country-Style Biscuits (p. 16), freshly baked
2 C. soy sausage, crumbled/chopped
3 T. canola oil
¼ C. flour
3 C. soy milk
¼ tsp. salt
¼ tsp. black pepper

Heat oil in a skillet over medium heat. Add soy sausage and cook until lightly browned. Sprinkle flour into skillet and stir, continuing to cook until flour stuck to soy sausage is browned. Add soy milk gradually, stirring constantly to ensure a smooth gravy until it thickens up. Stir in the salt and pepper and mix well

Split two or three Biscuits and spoon gravy overtop 'em, then dig in!

COUNTRY-FRIED TOFU

Greasy but tasty! You can serve this up by itself or on buns as a fried chicken-style patty.

½ C. oil
1 pkg. firm tofu, sliced 1 cm / 3/8 in. thick , pressed
    and marinated chicken-style (p. 7)
Southern-Fried Spice Mix (p. 10)
½ C. soy milk mixed with
    2 tsp. lemon juice
2 C. bread crumbs

Place spice mixture, soy milk mixture and bread crumbs in separate bowls

Heat oil in a large skillet over medium-high heat. Take each slice of tofu and dip it in the soy milk mixture, then the bread crumbs and finally the spice mixture before placing it in the skillet to cook in the hot oil. Cook each piece until browned, then flip it over and cook the other side 'til it's a nice golden brown too

Place cooked tofu slices on a plate lined with paper towels to blot out excess oil

SPAGHETTI SAUCE

This Spaghetti Sauce is a bit like one mah momma used to make – the whole cloves and cumin give it a richer flavor than what ya might get in a jar from yer local store

2 T. olive oil
1 onion, chopped
4 garlic cloves, minced
1 red bell pepper, chopped
1 C. mushrooms, chopped
2 carrots, peeled and chopped
1 stalk celery, chopped
3 cans peeled tomatoes and juice
½ C. tomato paste
2 tsp. salt
½ tsp. black pepper
1 tsp. dried basil
½ tsp. dried oregano
1 tsp. white sugar
¼ tsp. cumin
1 bay leaf
2 whole cloves (optional)

Heat olive oil in a large saucepan over medium heat. Sauté the onion and garlic a few minutes, until yer onion is translucent

Add remaining fresh chopped vegetables and sauté another few minutes

Stir in remaining ingredients, cover the pan and reduce the heat to a simmer

Simmer covered fer about an hour, stirring occasionally. Remove the bay leaf and whole cloves before serving over fresh pasta or steamed vegetables

SUN-DRIED TOMATO AND ARTICHOKE HEART LINGUINE

This might be some simple cookin', but it's still got a good flavor to it

2 T. olive oil
3 garlic cloves, chopped
2 tsp. dried oregano
2 tsp. dried basil
2 servings fresh cooked linguine
1 onion, chopped
1 C. sun-dried tomatoes, chopped
1 C. marinated artichoke hearts, chopped
Salt and cracked black pepper

Heat olive oil in a large saucepan or skillet over medium heat

Sauté the onion and garlic about five minutes, then add sun-dried tomatoes, basil and oregano

Stir until mixed well and heated up, then add the artichoke hearts. Stir well again and allow it all to cook until heated through

Serve over fresh cooked linguine with salt and black pepper added to suit yer taste

VEGETABLE MOUNTAIN WITH GRAVY

Sometimes a stack a' vegetables topped with tasty gravy is a perfect end to yer day

4 C. mashed potatoes, spiced to taste
Easy Gravy (p. 6)
2 T. oil
1 onion, sliced
2 carrots, sliced
1 red bell pepper, sliced
1 C. fresh mushrooms, sliced
2 C. fresh spinach, chopped
½ -1 tsp. dried basil
¼ tsp. dried parsley
1/8 tsp. dried rosemary
Salt and pepper to taste

Heat oil in a large skillet over medium heat and sauté onion a few minutes, then add carrots, mushrooms and spices

Sauté another five minutes, then add bell pepper and spinach and mix well

Sauté until the bell pepper is tender – cooked but still firm enough to snap

To serve, spoon some mashed potatoes in a mound on a plate and mash a pit in the middle of 'em. Fill it in with vegetables and top it all off with the gravy

VEGETABLE POT PIE

A hearty pie of tofu, vegetables and gravy inside a flaky crust ta fill ya up at dinner

2 Pie Crusts (p. 48)
2 C. Mushroom Gravy (p. 6)
¼ C. flour
1 tsp. salt
1/8 tsp. black pepper
1 T. nutritional yeast
¾ tsp. garlic powder
2 C. firm tofu, squeezed dry and cubed
2 T. oil
1 onion, chopped
1 carrot, chopped
1 stalk celery, sliced
1 C. frozen mixed vegetables

Preheat oven to 190° C/375° F. Line a pie plate with one of the pie crusts and bake for 10-15 minutes, until just starting to brown slightly

Combine flour, salt, pepper, nutritional yeast and garlic powder. Place in a paper bag or medium sized container with tofu and shake or toss well to coat tofu

Heat oil in a skillet over medium-high heat and sauté tofu until lightly browned, then add the onion, celery and carrot. Continue to sauté until the onions are soft, then add the mixed vegetables and cook until they're slightly tender but still crisp This should only take another 5-10 minutes - try snapping a green bean now and then to see how it's goin'

Add the gravy to mixture inta yer skillet and stir well, then transfer as much as will fit into the pie plate containing the baked pie crust

Cover it all up with the second, unbaked pie crust. Seal the edges by pressing 'em together with a fork or yer fingers, and cut a few slits in the top

Bake for 30 minutes in the preheated oven, or until top crust is lightly browned

VIETNAMESE-STYLE CURRY

A different kind a' curry than I normally make, but just as good as the rest. An Asian Grocery oughta have any of these ingredients ya can't find at yer usual grocery store.

1 T. oil
½ onion, chopped
1 green onion, sliced thin
1 clove garlic, chopped
2 T. fresh ginger root, sliced thin
1 stalk lemon grass, cut in pieces
2 T. curry powder
1 bay leaf
1 kaffir lime leaf, torn into pieces
½ green bell pepper, chopped
1 carrot, peeled and sliced diagonally
½ C. mushrooms, sliced
1 C. fried tofu, chopped
1 C. potatoes, chopped
1 can coconut milk
1 C. vegetable broth
1 C. water
1 tsp. red pepper flakes (to taste)
Fresh bean sprouts (garnish)
Fresh cilantro, chopped (garnish)
Cooked rice (for serving – optional)

Heat oil in a large stock pot over medium heat. Sauté onion and green onion until translucent then add garlic, ginger, lemon grass, curry, bay leaf and lime leaf

Stir together and cook for five minutes, then add in the bell pepper, carrots, mushrooms, tofu, vegetable broth and water. Stir well and bring to a boil

Add the potatoes and coconut milk, stir well and bring to a boil again. Reduce heat and simmer 45 minutes or until it reduces and potatoes are cooked

Serve in bowls or over rice, with bean sprouts and chopped cilantro fer garnish

VEGETABLE AND TOFU CURRY

An easy curry of tofu and vegetables, with some fresh spices ta give it a kick

1 pkg. firm tofu, squeezed dry and cubed
1 C. green onions, chopped with green tops reserved
1 can coconut milk
2 C. fresh tomatoes, seeded and chopped
1 red bell pepper, sliced
4 C. bok choy, chopped
½ C. mushrooms, chopped
¼-½ C. fresh basil, chopped
¼ C. soy sauce
½ tsp. brown sugar
1 ½ tsp. curry powder
1 tsp. fresh ginger, minced
2 tsp. red chili paste
Salt and pepper (to taste)
Cooked rice (for serving - optional)

In a skillet over medium-heat, combine coconut milk, soy sauce, brown sugar, curry powder, ginger and chili paste. Bring to a boil then stir in tofu, green onions, tomatoes, red bell pepper, and mushrooms

Cover and cook for about five minutes, stirring occasionally. Add fresh basil and bok choy along with salt and pepper to taste. Continue cooking until vegetables are tender (cooked but still crisp enough to snap), about another five minutes

Serve in bowls or on rice, garnished with the chopped green onions tops

44

COCONUT CURRY TOFU ON GREEN JASMINE RICE

It might take a bit of work, but you'll be rarin' ta go n' make it again once ya taste it

1 C. uncooked jasmine rice
1 ¾ C. water
1 tsp. salt
¼ C. shredded coconut, toasted
1 C. fresh parsley or cilantro, chopped
1 can coconut milk
4 tsp. fresh ginger, minced
1 T. lime juice
¼ tsp. black pepper
2 cloves garlic, minced
2 T. vegetable oil
2 C. firm tofu, squeezed dry and cubed
½ C. green onions, thinly sliced
2 tsp. curry powder
1 tsp. cumin
¼ tsp. crushed dried red pepper flakes
1 can chopped tomatoes + juice
2 T. chopped peanuts (garnish)

Bring water and salt to boil in a medium-sized saucepan and stir in jasmine rice. Return the water to a boil then reduce the heat and simmer covered until the water is absorbed and rice is tender, about 20 minutes

Puree parsley/cilantro, ½ C. coconut milk, 1 tsp. ginger, lime juice, pepper and half of the garlic together in a blender or food processor. Mix the puree and coconut inta yer cooked jasmine rice, then cover and set it aside fer later

Heat oil in a large skillet over high heat and add the tofu. Stir-fry until golden brown, about five minutes - keep it movin' to prevent any burnin'

Add onions, spices, and remaining ginger and garlic. Stir-fry fer a minute or so, then stir in the remaining coconut milk and the chopped tomatoes, and heat it all through. Add more salt and pepper at this point ta suit yer taste

Serve over the green jasmine rice and garnish with chopped peanuts

DESSERTS

QUICK CAKE FROSTING

A simple frosting ya kin flavor however ya like for cakes (p.52 and 53)

2 C. powdered sugar
½ C. margarine
¼ tsp. salt
2 T. water
½ tsp. liquid for flavor (vanilla, lemon juice, coffee, rum, etc.)

In a large bowl combine all of the ingredients. More sugar or water may be
needed depending upon how thick you want the frosting ta be

CHOCOLATE CAKE FROSTING

Tasty, fudgey frosting that'll suit just about any cake, birthday or otherwise (p.52 and 53)

3 C. sifted powdered sugar
5 T. water, divided
1 tsp. vanilla extract
2/3 C. cocoa
½ C. margarine, softened

Beat 1 C. sugar, 2 T. water, and remaining ingredients together until creamy.
Gradually beat in remaining sugar and water until smooth then get ta frostin'!

DESERVE'S
GOT NOTHIN'
TO DO WITH
IT.

46

CREAM CHEESE-STYLE FROSTING

A Cream Cheese type frosting ta slap onta yer Carrot Cake (p.59) or whatever ya like

¼ C. almonds, peeled and ground (or just use almond meal)
1 C. water
2 T. lemon juice
2 T. cornstarch
1 ½ T. canola oil
½ tsp. nutritional yeast
¼ salt (or slightly less)
½ C. white sugar
1 tsp. vanilla extract

Use a blender ta blend the ground almonds with half the water (½ C.) until it forms a smooth mixture. Add the remaining water and all ingredients except the sugar and vanilla. Blend on high speed until the mixture is smooth and creamy

Pour into a medium saucepan and bring to a boil over medium-high heat, stirring constantly to prevent scorching. Once mixture thickens, reduce heat and simmer for another minute or two, continuing to stir

Remove saucepan from heat and beat in the sugar and vanilla extract, then let it stand for awhile ta cool

Once mixture has cooled, beat well with a whisk or electric beater to get a smooth consistency. Transfer to a container and chill it in the refrigerator, where it'll thicken up a bit more. Beat well again before usin', to make it more spreadable

47

CARAMEL TOPPING

It takes a bit of time, but you'll have a caramel sauce to use for ice cream, cakes or as an essential ingredient in recipes like Caramel and Cranberry Date Bars (p.51)

2 C. soy milk
1 C. powdered sugar
3 T. margarine
a toothpick and ink pen

Pour 1 C. soy milk into a small saucepan. Dip the toothpick straight down in the saucepan until it touches bottom. Use the ink pen to mark height of the soymilk on yer toothpick – now you've got a measuring stick for reducing. Add remaining soy milk to the saucepan and bring to a boil. Reduce heat and simmer until it reduces to the level marked on yer toothpick, about 20-25 minutes. Stir regularly and watch to prevent boilover – briefly lift off heat and stir if that's gonna happen.

Add the powdered sugar and margarine, stirring well until sugar is dissolved and margarine melted. Reduce heat to barely simmering, and continue heating and stirring another 15-20 min. until color is darker brown and it starts to thicken – it will thicken more as it cools. Remove from heat and use warm or refrigerate for later (just warm it up slightly and stir well before usin')

PIE CRUST

A flaky crust that'll come in handy mostly for desserts (p. 60 and 61) but you it's good fer dinner pies (p.42) too. Add herbs or spices in with the flour fer a bit of extra flavor.

¾ C. sifted flour
¼ C. margarine
1/8 tsp. salt
2 T. ice water

❦ If you place the measured ingredients in a freezer for 20 minutes beforehand, it'll make the crust a bit easier ta work with when it's mixed

Mix flour and salt together, then cut in margarine with two knives or a pastry blender. Add the ice water and mix well, kneading with hands if necessary to ensure there are no pockets of dry flour. Form the dough into a ball and roll out on a lightly floured surface to form your pie crust, then put it to good use!

GREAT GRANDMA CARLSON'S APPLE CRISP
Like lotsa great food this is a family recipe, passed on to me by some fine folks I know

1 C. brown sugar
1 tsp. salt
1 C. rolled oats
1 ¼ C. sifted flour
¼ C. orange juice
2/3 C. margarine
1 C. rhubarb, chopped
2 C. granny smith apples, peeled, cored and chopped

Preheat oven to 190° C/375° F. Lightly grease the bottom of a 9x13 baking pan with non-stick spray or margarine. Combine dry ingredients and mix well, then cut in margarine with two knives or a pastry blender until margarine is pea-sized or smaller. Spread chopped fruit into pan and drizzle with orange juice. Sprinkle oat mixture on top and bake for 30-40 minutes. Serve warm

SPICED ICE CREAM
Try on Pancakes (p. 17), Apple Pie (p. 60), Apple Enchiladas(p. 58) or just on its own

3 C. soy milk
¾ C. sugar
1 T. vanilla extract
½ tsp. allspice
1 can coconut milk
1/3 C. apple juice
1 T. cinnamon
¼ t. nutmeg

Whisk all ingredients together in a large bowl and pour inta a shallow pan that'll fit in yer freezer. Place the pan in the freezer and stir at hourly intervals ta ensure a smooth texture until it's totally frozen. Thaw slightly, stir and transfer to an airtight storage container keep frozen until yer ready ta use it

COFFEE CAKE BARS

These'll spice up a cold morning on the plains and get ya ready for some wranglin'

1 ¼ C. white sugar
¾ C. brown sugar
2 C. flour
½ C. margarine, softened
½ C. shredded coconut
½ C. chopped walnuts
1 tsp. baking soda
½ tsp. salt
1 tsp. ground cinnamon
2 egg substitutes
1 tsp. vanilla extract
1 C. soy milk mixed with
    1 T. lemon juice
1 C. powdered sugar
1-2 T. water

Preheat oven to 175° C/350° F and grease a 9x13 baking pan with margarine or non-stick cooking spray

In a medium bowl, blend sugars, flour and margarine with a pastry blender or two knives until mixture is coarse crumbs. Move 2 C. of the mixture to another bowl and set the rest aside. Stir the coconut and walnuts into the 2 C. of crumb mixture and press firmly into the bottom of the greased baking pan

Stir the baking soda, salt and cinnamon into the bowl of saved crumb mixture. Add the egg substitutes, vanilla and soymilk, mixing until well blended. Pour this over the crumb base ya already pressed into the baking pan. Bake 35-45 minutes in the preheated oven, until set and a bit spongy

Allow to cool, then mix the powdered sugar and water together to make a glaze. Add water gradually to reach a consistency yer happy with, then drizzle it onto the cake. Allow yer glaze to set before cuttin' the cake inta bars

CRANBERRY AND CARAMEL DATE BARS

This odd combination of cranberries, dates and caramel winds up tastin' amazing

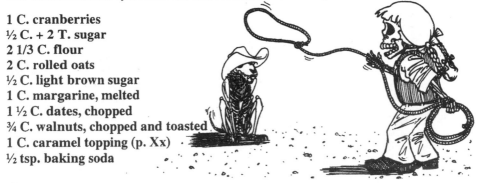

1 C. cranberries
½ C. + 2 T. sugar
2 1/3 C. flour
2 C. rolled oats
½ C. light brown sugar
1 C. margarine, melted
1 ½ C. dates, chopped
¾ C. walnuts, chopped and toasted
1 C. caramel topping (p. Xx)
½ tsp. baking soda

✪ If yer using whole dates, they chop easier with kitchen scissors or a knife sprayed with non-stick cooking spray

✪ Rehydrate dried cranberries by soaking them in water for about an hour

Preheat oven to 175° C/350° F. In a small bowl, combine cranberries and 2 T. white sugar. In a separate, large bowl combine 2 C. flour, oats, remaining sugars and baking soda. Add margarine and mix well. Set aside 1 C. of the mixture and press the rest firmly into the bottom of a 9x13 baking pan. Bake for 15 minutes

Get yer crust out've the oven and sprinkle on the dates, walnuts and cranberries

Mix caramel topping with remaining 1/3 C. flour and spoon it overtop the fruit and nuts. Then cover that with the remaining 1 C. of base mixture and bake another 20 minutes or until lightly brown. Give it some time ta cool before cuttin'

ASIAN COCONUT RICE

An easy dessert ya might want ta use for roundin' out meals with curries (p. 43-45)

1 can coconut milk
1 ¼ C. water
1 T. sugar
1/8 tsp. salt
1 ½ C. jasmine rice, uncooked
Shredded coconut, toasted (garnish)
Sprigs of fresh cilantro (garnish)

In a saucepan, combine coconut milk, water, sugar and salt. Stir until sugar is dissolved, then stir in the rice. Bring it all to a boil over medium heat, then cover and reduce heat and simmer about 20 minutes until rice is tender. Garnish with toasted shredded coconut and sprigs of fresh cilantro

VANILLA (YELLOW) CAKE

This'll work as a cake for birthdays or any other occasion – frost this puppy up! (p. 46)

2 C. flour
1 T. baking powder
1 tsp. salt
1 ½ C. white sugar
½ C. margarine
4 egg substitutes
1 C. soy milk
1 tsp. vanilla extract
1/8 tsp. almond extract (optional)

Preheat oven to 175° C/350° F. Grease and flour a 9x13 pan or two 23 cm/9 in. round pans. Sift flour, baking powder and salt together in a bowl and set aside

In a large bowl, mix sugar and margarine together until creamed to a light and fluffy consistency. Add egg substitutes and mix well. Alternate adding the flour mixture and soy milk, stirring well after each addition but not overmixin'. Stir in the vanilla extract and almond extract, then pour batter into prepared pan(s)

Bake 35-45 minutes, until a toothpick or knife inserted into center comes out clean. Allow to cool before removing it from yer pan(s) or frosting it

CHOCOLATE CAKE

A general-purpose (chocolate variety) cake that ya kin top off with frostings (p.46)

1 ½ C. flour
1 C. white sugar
1 tsp. baking soda
1 C. cold water
¼ C. + 1 T. oil or applesauce
1 tsp. salt
¼ cocoa
1 tsp. vanilla extract
1 T. white vinegar
½ C. semi-sweet chocolate bits (optional)
¼ C. chopped walnuts (optional)

Preheat oven to 175° C/350° F and grease a 20 cm/8 in. square baking pan with margarine or non-stick cooking spray and lightly dust with flour

Combine dry ingredients in a large bowl and mix well. Stir in oil, vinegar and vanilla. When mix is completely moistened, pour in water and stir until smooth

Fold in the chocolate bits and nuts if ya want 'em, and pour the batter into the pan

Bake in yer preheated oven 30-35 minutes until a toothpick or knife inserted into the center comes out clean. Allow it ta cool before slappin' on any frosting

MIGHTY CHEWY BROWNIES

For as easy as they are to whip up, these are some mighty fine chewy brownies

¾ C. margarine, melted
1 2/3 C. granulated sugar
2 T. water
2 egg substitutes
2 tsp. vanilla extract
¾ C. cocoa
1 1/3 C. flour
½ tsp. Baking powder
¼ tsp. Salt
¾ C. chopped nuts (optional)

Preheat oven to 175° C/350° F.

Stir margarine, sugar and water together in a medium-sized bowl, then add the egg substitutes and vanilla extract

In a separate bowl, combine the dry ingredients except nuts and mix well

Stir the cocoa mixture into the sugar mixture a bit at a time to avoid dry clumps in yer batter, then fold in the nuts if you're optin' to use them

Spread batter in an ungreased 9x13 baking pan and bake for 20-25 minutes

They're done when a toothpick stuck into the center comes out slightly sticky but fairly clean. Whatever else ya might do, don't overcook these suckers - you'll wind up with a cocoa brick that'll just about break yer teeth off!

STAMPEDE COOKIES

With so much chucked inta these cookies, ah can't quite decide what kind they are, but the result is a good 'un – add or subtract ingredients ta suit yer own taste

1 C. margarine
¾ C. white sugar
¾ C. brown sugar
2 egg substitutes
1 tsp. vanilla extract
2 ¼ C. flour
½ tsp. salt
1 tsp. baking soda
¼ tsp. baking powder
½ C. rolled oats
1 C. chocolate chips/chunks
½ C. walnuts, chopped
½ C. shredded coconut

Preheat oven to 190° C/375° F.

In a large bowl, mix margarine, sugars, egg substitutes and vanilla until creamy
In a separate bowl, combine the flour, salt, baking soda and baking powder

Stir the flour mixture into the sugar mixture until ingredients are well blended

Stir in remaining ingredients and mix well. Drop dough by the spoonful onto an ungreased cookie sheet and bake fer 12-15 minutes, until lightly browned

Allow to cool before removing from the cookie sheet, and don't fergit ta "test" a few – wouldn't want yer gang windin' up with any bad cookies, now would ya?

VANILLA FUDGE

Sure it's a bit complicated, but local folk couldn't tell this wasn't "real", so it's a keeper

4 ¼ C. white sugar
1 ¼ C. soy milk
1 C. margarine
2 tsp. vanilla extract
pan of cold water (for use later)
½ C. chopped nuts (any kind, optional)

Grease a 20 cm/8 in. square baking pan with margarine or non-stick cooking spray

In a large saucepan over low to medium heat, bring the soy milk to a boil. Add the sugar and margarine and continue heating, stirring constantly with a wooden spoon until sugar dissolves and margarine melts

Bring the mixture to a boil then lower heat slightly (still boiling) and cover the pan. Boil this way for two minutes, keeping a close eye on it in case a' boilover

Uncover and continue boiling until it reaches the "soft-ball stage", which ya kin test for as follows. If you've got a sugar thermometer this'll be 115° C/238° F, but fer those of us not so lucky it can be a bit tricky. Basically the mixture should still be watery and at a fast boil. When you take a small amount of it on your spoon and drop it in the pan of cold water, it should turn to a jelly-like blob that's slightly firm but still mashes between yer fingers – a "soft ball" like the name sez

Once you've reached that stage, remove the mixture from heat and stir in the vanilla. Set aside for about five minutes to cool slightly, then beat until the mixture loses it's glossy surface and thickens up to an almost batter-like texture. Use an electric mixer if ya got one pardner, or ya could be there all day!

Stir in chopped nuts if yer usin' 'em, and pour it all into yer greased square pan and chill in the refrigerator or freezer for a few hours before cutting

CHOCOLATE FUDGE

An altogether different kind a' fudge than yer vanilla variety, and not quite as complicated

2 C. soy milk
1 C. powdered sugar
3 C. chocolate chips/chunks
1/8 tsp. salt
1 ½ tsp. vanilla extract
1 C. chopped nuts (optional)
toothpick and ink pen

Grease a 20 cm/8 in. square baking pan with margarine or non-stick cooking spray

Pour 1 C. soy milk into a small saucepan. Dip the toothpick straight down in the saucepan until it touches bottom and use the ink pen to mark height the soymilk reached on the toothpick – this'll be yer measuring stick for reducing the soymilk

Add remaining soy milk to the saucepan and bring it to a boil. Reduce the heat and simmer until it reduces to the height you marked on yer toothpick, should take about 20-25 minutes. Stir regularly and watch to prevent boilover – briefly lift the saucepan off the heat and stir if that's gonna happen, then return to the burner

Lower heat and add sugar, stirring until completely dissolved. Add chocolate and salt, stirring until chocolate melts and a smooth consistency forms

Remove from heat and stir in vanilla and nuts, then pour into prepared square pan. Chill in the refrigerator or freezer for a few hours until firm before cutting

APPLE ENCHILADAS

A tasty excuse to use any leftover tortillas – try toppin' with Spiced Ice Cream (p. 49)

6 flour tortillas (p. 12)
½ C. white sugar
½ C. brown sugar
1/3 C. water
1 tsp. ground cinnamon
½ C. margarine
4 C. apple pie filling, canned or ya kin make as follows:
- 4 granny smith apples, peeled, cored and sliced
- 3/4 C. white sugar
- 3/4 C. brown sugar
- 1 ½ tsp. ground cinnamon
- 1/8 tsp. nutmeg

Preheat oven to 175° C/350° F and grease a 20 cm/8 in. square baking pan

Place a few heaped spoonfuls of filling in each tortilla, then roll the tortillas up and place 'em in the baking pan, seam-side down

Heat water, sugars, margarine and cinnamon in a saucepan over medium heat. Bring to a boil, stirring constantly to prevent burning. Reduce heat and simmer for a few minutes to let sauce thicken. Remove from heat and pour over tortillas, spreading with a spoon to ensure they are evenly coated

Bake in the oven fer 20 minutes, until bubblin' and golden brown on top

CARROT CAKE

A hefty carrot cake topped with Cream Cheese Style Frosting ta take care a' yer dessert

2 C. flour
1 tsp. baking soda
1 T. baking powder
¼ tsp. salt
1 tsp. ground cinnamon
3 egg substitutes
½ C. soymilk mixed with
    2 tsp. lemon juice
2 T. oil or applesauce
1 C. white sugar
2 tsp. vanilla extract
1 ½ C. carrots, peeled and shredded
½ C. flaked/desiccated coconut (optional)
½ C. chopped walnuts (optional)
½ C. raisins (optional)
½ C. crushed pineapple, drained (optional)
Cream Cheese Style Frosting (p. 47)

Preheat oven to 175C° /350° F and grease a 20 cm/8 in. square baking pan

Sift the flour, baking soda, baking powder, salt and ground cinnamon together in a small bowl and set aside

In a large bowl, combine egg substitutes, soymilk mixture, oil, sugar and vanilla. Mix well, then add bowl of spiced flour and mix until well blended

In another bowl, combine carrots, coconut, walnuts, raisins and pineapple. Stir well to evenly distribute, then fold it inta the large bowl of batter. Pour into greased pan and bake in preheated oven 35-40 minutes, until a toothpick inserted in the center comes out clean

Let cool before applyin' Cream Cheese Style Frosting, then chill before serving

APPLE PIE

It's about as old-fashioned as pies get – try it topped with Spiced Ice Cream (p. 49) to serve it a` la mode (not 'Alamo', mind you – that's another matter altogether)

2 unbaked pie crusts (p. 48)
½ C. white sugar
¼ C. flour
½ C. packed brown sugar
1 tsp. ground cinnamon
¼ tsp. ground nutmeg
5 granny smith apples, peeled, cored and sliced thin

Preheat oven to 190° C/375° F and line a pie plate with one a' the pie crusts

In a large bowl, combine sugars, flour and spices. Add apples and toss well. Pou the apple mixture into the pie plate, then cover it all with yer second pie crust, press the edges together with a fork and cut a few vents in the top

Place on a baking sheet (to catch any spillover) in the preheated oven. Cook for 55 minutes, until filling bubbles and the apples are cooked

PUMPKIN PIE

Just about the best thing yu kin ask from a pumpkin, besides fresh Pumpkin Bread (p.19)

1 unbaked pie crust (p. 48)
2 C. pumpkin, cooked and pureed
¾ C. white or brown sugar
1 tsp. ground cinnamon
¼ tsp. ground cloves
½ C. silken tofu, squeezed and pureed
½ tsp. salt
½ tsp. ground ginger

Preheat the oven to 220° C/425° F and line a pie plate with the unbaked pie crust. Blend all ingredients together and pour into the pie plate lined with crust

Cook at 220° C/425° F for 15 minutes, then reduce heat to 175° C/350° F and cook an additional 45 minutes until it's firm. Chill in refrigerator before servin'

SWEET POTATO PIE

Not a flavor of pie you'd expect, but once ya have a taste it'll make perfect sense to ya

1 unbaked pie crust (p. 48)
1 ½ C. sweet potato, cooked and mashed
1 T. margarine, softened
1 tsp. baking powder
1/8 tsp. ground cloves
1/8 tsp. ground nutmeg
½ C. silken tofu, squeezed and pureed
1 C. white sugar
1 tsp. baking soda
1 tsp. ground cinnamon
1/8 tsp. ground allspice
½ tsp. vanilla extract
½ C. soy milk with
    2 tsp. lemon juice mixed in

Preheat oven to 200° C/400° F and line a pie plate with the unbaked crust.
In a large bowl, combine sweet potato, margarine and dry ingredients. Beat until smooth, then stir in tofu, soy milk and vanilla

Pour into pie plate and bake in preheated oven at 200° C/400° F for 10 minutes, then reduce heat to 175° C/350° F and cook an additional 35 minutes. Serve warm or chilled and garnished with whipped topping and a whole pecan

~ADIOS, MUCHACHOS.~

THE DIRTY SOUTH

The recipes in this book were compiled from 4 separate zines - 3 issues of the *Dirty South* cook zine (including one that was never published) and one issue of *Hot Damn & Hell Yeah*. The idea came up in a meeting about four years ago to publish it as one book, with the *Dirty South* side upside down, to be read as two different books.

In hindsight, this may not have been the best choice. It seemed to confuse people that it was setup that way on purpose and we were accused more than once of misprinting the last half.

Many of the critical reviews of this book seemed to discredit the *Dirty South* half, partially due to the "flip" split style of the first two editions of this book and partially due to poor editing of the recipes. With these criticisms in mind, we've edited the recipes again, done new layout for this half and sought out new illustrations from Sarah Oleksyk.

We've also done away with the "flip" format and made it appear more like a typical book. We hope to make Vanessa's incredible recipes more accessible and easier to use.

Enjoy!

Thanks!
Microcosm

THE DIRTY SOUTH

A FEW THINGS
ABOUT THIS BOOK

This is Dirty South, even though I ain't in the south no more. These recipes aren't meant to be used every day. There are lots of vegan cookbooks out there for those who are interested in veganism for health or ethical reasons.

Those books usually have pretty good guidelines as to what you should eat a lot of (fruits, vegetables, grains, blah) and what you should not eat a lot of (fat, sweets, etc.).

That's not really what this is about. There are recipes that I think are proof that you CAN make good southern food without meat.

Most of these recipes are also really cheap to make, and easy and fun too.

Thanks for reading.
Xxx Vanessa J. Mazuz // amalgamationcake@gmail.com

Thanks:
Yoni, Willie, Natalia, Yvette's aunt Kathy, my grandmother, and everyone who eats whatever I put in front of them. http://paku-paku.info, the Post Punk Kitchen, Frankie Lymon, New Orleans, and lily. Oh and PLF.

OIL

A bit about cooking oil:

Most of these recipes require cooking oil. Canola oil works best because it can withstand high heat and really doesn't have a flavor of its own. Corn oil is okay too, but I think it's higher in saturated fat. Olive oil is really no good for most of these recipes because it has a pretty strong flavor, which you will taste in whatever you're cooking. Never try to deep fry anything in margarine because it will burn or you'll burn yourself. Okay, enough about that.

TABLE OF CONTENTS

BREADS

MAIN DISHES

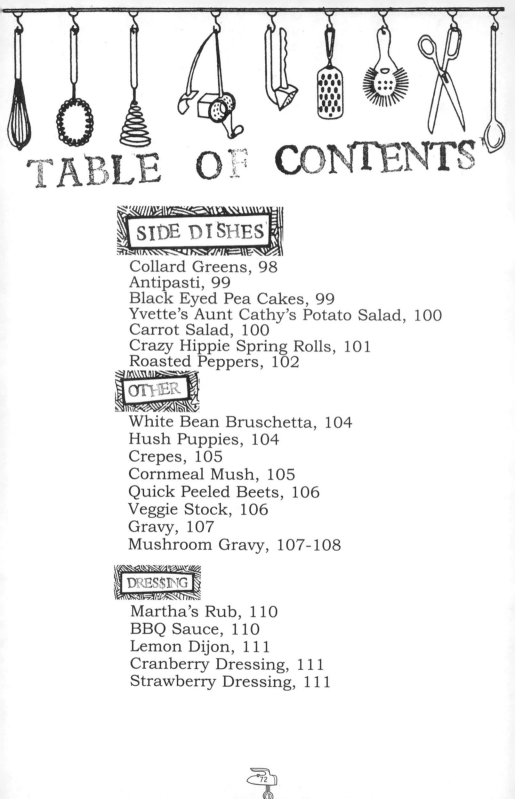

TABLE OF CONTENTS

SIDE DISHES

OTHER

DRESSING

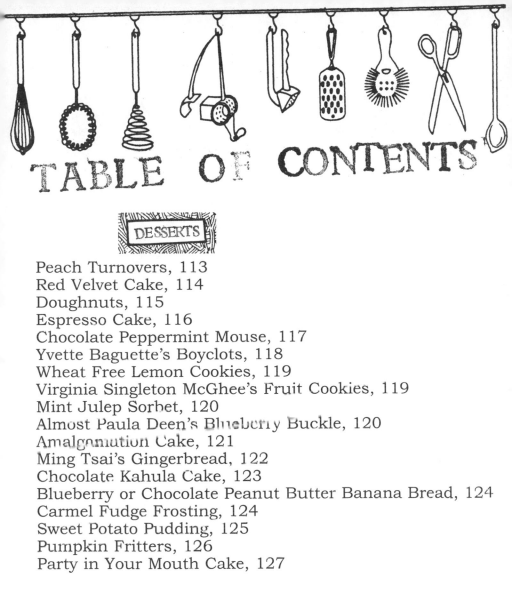

TABLE OF CONTENTS

DESSERTS

BREADS

CURRANT SCONES

Ingredients:
1 C. flour
1 C. wheat pastry flour
¼ C. sugar
1 T. baking powder
½ tsp. salt
6 T. margarine
½ C. currants
1 tsp. orange or lemon zest
1 tsp. vanilla

Mix together the first 5 ingredients. Then cut in the margarine with 2 knives (or a pastry cutter) until the mixture is crumbly and all margarine is mixed in. Add the currants, then add the soymilk, vanilla and lemon zest. Mix until all ingredients are combined. Form the dough into a ball and knead for a few minutes, then pat the dough out and cut into wedges. Place on a baking sheet and brush with soymilk, then sprinkle tops with sugar. Bake at 425° F for about 25 minutes.

You can substitute chocolate chips for the currants, if you want!

QUICK YEAST BREAD

Ingredients:
2 C. flour
1 T. sugar
1 ¼ tsp. salt
1 package of quick-rising active dry yeast
1 C. warm water
2 T. vegetable oil
1 C. flour

Combine the first four ingredients. Slowly add the warm water and vegetable oil. Mix for a minute, then add flour. Knead the dough for about 10 minutes, place in a greased bowl and cover. Let the dough rise for about 30 minutes. Punch down the dough (flour your hands before you do this) and form into a loaf. Place in a greased pan, cover and let rise another 30 minutes. While it is rising, preheat the oven to 450° F. After the dough has risen again, bake at 450° F for 10 minutes, then reduce heat to 350° F and bake for about 30 minutes. Don't cool the bread in the pan—take it out and cool it on a rack.

MORE PIZZA DOUGH THAN YOU'LL EVER NEED

Ingredients:
25 lbs. flour
4 oz. salt
14 oz. sugar
5 oz. olive oil
1 pound melted vegetable shortening
½ oz. yeast
1 C. hot water
about 8 C. cold water, plus another 9 C. later

I used to work as a pizza cook, so the only pizza dough recipe I know makes about thirty pizzas. If you don't have access to a Hobart mixer, maybe you can figure out how to pare it down.

Put all of your flour into a huge mixer. Add the salt, sugar, and olive oil, then the melted vegetable shortening. Sprinkle yeast over hot water. When yeast mixture is dissolved, add to other ingredients. Turn on mixer at low speed and slowly add your cold water. Keep adding water until the dough seems the right consistency (about 17 C. total) and switch to medium speed. Mix the dough for about 30 minutes then place in a bag, tie shut and let rise overnight (or, at least 8 hours).

BUTTERMILK BISCUITS

Ingredients:
2 C. flour
1 T. baking powder
1 heaping spoonful nutritional yeast
1 T. sugar or honey
1 tsp. salt
⅓ C. oil
⅔ C. soy milk mixed with a spoonful or two of vinegar

Combine dry ingredients. Add oil and soymilk and stir well. Drop large spoonfuls onto a greased baking sheet and bake at 450° F for 15-20 minutes.

These definitely don't last long, and are the best eaten right out of the oven (with gravy, of course) unless you want to use them to play kickball.

SPELT BISCUITS

Ingredients:
1 ⅔ C. spelt flour
1 T. baking powder
½ tsp. salt
⅔ C. soymilk
⅓ C. canola oil

In a large bowl, combine dry ingredients. Then in another bowl, mix together the soymilk and oil and add to the flour mixture. Stir just until all is combined well. The dough will be thick and sticky—don't try to make it smooth. Drop the dough in spoonfuls onto an ungreased baking sheet and bake at 475° F for about 8-10 minutes.

CORNBREAD

Ingredients:
1 ¼ C. flour
¾ C. cornmeal
½ C. sugar
2 tsp. baking powder
½ tsp. salt
1 C. soymilk
¼ C. vegetable oil or margarine
2 T. arrowroot, mixed with 1/4 cup apple sauce
½-1 C. corn
optional– some rosemary

Combine the dry ingredients. Add everything else and stir just until it's all combined. Pour the batter into a greased pan and bake at 400° F for about 25 minutes.

Test by sticking a fork or toothpick into the center – it should come out mostly clean.

SUMER'S FRY BREAD

Ingredients:
2 ½ C. un-yeasted white flour
1 ½ T. baking powder
1 tsp. salt
¾ C. of warm water
1 T. vegetable oil
1 T. soymilk
vegetable oil for frying

Combine flour, baking powder and salt in a large bowl.
Combine water, oil and soymilk and stir into flour mixture
until smooth dough forms. Turn out onto lightly floured surface. Knead 4 times into smooth ball. Cover and let rest 10
minutes. Divide dough into 8 balls. Flatten with fingertips or
roll out each ball 8 to 10 inches round. Make a small hole in
the center of each with finger or handle of wooden spoon.

Lightly flour rounds, stack and cover with towel or plastic
wrap. Heat about an inch of oil in a large skillet. Gently place
bread rounds one at a time in hot oil and cook till crispy and
golden, one to two minutes on each side, depending on thickness. Drain on paper towels. Serve bread hot or at room temperature.

CORNMEAL FRY BREAD

Ingredients:
1 C. cornmeal
1 C. flour
4 tsp. baking powder
egg replacer for 1 egg
¼ C. oil
about 1 C. milk or equivalent
vegetable oil for frying

Whisk together dry ingredients in a bowl. Make a well in the
center and add the liquid. Mix just until combined; the batter should be thick like cornbread batter, but thin enough
that you can spread it around the hot skillet. Fry one at a
time, by dropping the batter in a very hot skillet with about
⅛" of oil in the bottom, and spreading batter around quickly.
You can't form these into balls like the previous kind.

Ingredients:
2 T. finely chopped fresh rosemary
1 ½ C. flour
1 C. sugar
a pinch of salt
1 tsp. baking powder
1 stick unsalted margarine
egg replacer for 2 eggs
1 C. liquid soy creamer
1 C. dried fruit (currants, chopped figs, etc.)

Combine dry ingredients, and cut margarine into dry ingredients. Add rosemary, then everything else. Roll out or just drop by spoonfuls (my method) onto baking pan. Brush with water or soy milk and sprinkle with sugar. Bake at 350° F for 10-15 minutes. Serve with lemon curd or vanilla ice cream (or both!)

JOHNNY CAKES

My grandmother had seven kids and seventeen grand-kids, so whenever we would all visit her, she made this.

It's really incredibly cheap to make and feeds massive amounts of people.

Ingredients:
3 C. flour
3 tsp. baking powder
1 heaping tsp. salt
1-2 T. sugar
½ C. soy milk*
½ C. water*

*You can use all soy milk or all water, it's up to you—just so long as the total liquid amounts to 1 C.

Mix the dry ingredients together. Add the liquid until you get a dough that resembles bread dough. Coat your hands with flour and knead the dough into a ball for a few minutes.

Put the dough ball into a greased bowl and cover with a warm damp cloth. Let this sit for any time between 30 minutes and 3 hours. After it sits, take the dough and put it on a floured surface. Roll out (if you don't have a rolling pin, a Boone's bottle works really well) to about ½-inch thickness. Use the mouth of a drinking glass to cut the dough into circles.

The remaining pieces can be shaped into balls, or what-ever pleases you.

Deep fry in oil till the Johnny cakes puff up and are brown on both sides.

MAIN DISHES

SEITAN

Ingredients:
1 ½ C. vital wheat gluten
¼ C. nutritional yeast
¼ tsp. garlic powder
1 T. unsalted poultry seasoning
½ tsp. thyme
¼ tsp. onion powder
1 C. vegetable stock (pg. 106)
2-3 T. soy sauce
1 T. oil

Separately:
10 C. vegetable stock or water
½ C. soy sauce
onions, chopped
mushrooms
carrots
carrot tops
green onions
garlic, chopped
bell pepper

Put the wheat gluten, nutritional yeast, and spices into a bowl and stir them together.

Add the first measurement of vegetable stock, soy sauce and oil to the dry ingredients.

Mix until you have a firm and spongy sort of dough. You might have to add a few tablespoons of water to get all the wheat gluten mixed into dough. Knead the dough for a minute, then cut into a few big chunks and set aside.

Now, place 10 C. of vegetable stock (or water) and ½ C. soy sauce into a large pot. Add the vegetables (this is all for seasoning the seitan) and the gluten dough. Bring this to a boil, then partially cover and cook it at very low temperature for about an hour. Let the seitan pieces cool in the pot before using or refrigerating. Store the seitan in broth or water and use it within a week.

If you're feeding more than 4 people you should probably double this recipe.

SEITAN DIRTY RICE

Ingredients:
2 C. rice
4 C. vegetable stock
4 cloves chopped garlic
1 C. chopped onion
1-2 bell peppers, chopped
vegetable oil
salt, pepper, thyme
¼ tsp. cayenne
1 bay leaf
1 bunch green onions, chopped
2 C. seitan, chopped or ground (whatever's easier)

Rinse rice, then put in a pot with vegetable stock. Bring to a boil, then simmer for 20 minutes. Sauté garlic, onions, and peppers in oil until soft. Add salt, pepper, thyme, bay leaf, and cayenne. Add the green onions and seitan and cook for a few more minutes. Add this to the rice and cook till it's done. Taste for seasoning.

FAKE FRIED CHICKEN

So this actually tastes more like country-fried steak, but it kind of looks and smells like fried chicken, hence the name.

Ingredients for breading:
seitan (pg. 84), cut into chicken-sized chunks (you know what I mean)
½ C. flour
½ C. cornmeal
¼ C. nutritional yeast
¼ tsp. cayenne pepper
1 tsp. salt or Cajun seasoning
¼ tsp. garlic powder
¼ tsp. pepper

Ingredients for batter:
½ C. soymilk
½ C. flour
3 to 4 T. Creole mustard
salt and pepper to taste

First combine flour and cornmeal, then add yeast and spices. This is your breading. In a separate bowl, combine the soymilk and flour with Creole mustard, salt and pepper to make a thick batter. You may need to adjust the flour/soymilk measurements a little. Take the seitan pieces and dip them in the batter, then in the breading. Fry in canola oil until brown on both sides. This is best served with mashed potatoes, greens, cornbread and iced tea.

FRIED POTATOES

Ingredients:
1 large tomato, diced
4-6 potatoes
½ lb. of tofu
½ lb. mushrooms
1 yellow onion
1 bell pepper
1 bunch green onions
a few garlic cloves
Cajun seasoning to taste—or make your own by combining cayenne, salt, pepper, garlic powder, onion powder and chili powder.

Wash the potatoes well and dice. You don't need to take the skins off. Heat some oil in a sauce pan, add the potatoes, garlic, and spices and cook until the potatoes are about half done. Chop the vegetables and add to the potatoes. Add a little bit of water if the potatoes start to stick. Cook until the potatoes are soft and the vegetables are done.

Note: Yukon gold potatoes are the best potatoes ever—but you can use baking potatoes too, or red potatoes...

BBQ TOFU

Ingredients:
2 lbs. extra firm tofu
1 onion
1 bell pepper
1 large carrot
4 mushrooms
3 cloves of garlic
small can of tomato paste
3 T. ketchup
1 bottle BBQ sauce (yeah I'm lazy)
¼ tsp. garlic powder
1 tsp. vegan Worcestershire sauce, if you can get it
1 tsp. soy sauce or Braggs
1 T. brown sugar

First press the water out of the tofu. Cut the tofu into big pieces and place on a baking sheet, or flat surface.

Put a heavy weight on top of the tofu (like a pot full of cans of vegetables) and let the water drain out of it for about 20 minutes.

While the tofu is draining, chop all the vegetables and garlic. Put in a pot with some oil or margarine, add the spices and cook until onions are soft.

Add the BBQ sauce, tomato paste, brown sugar, ketchup and soy sauce (and the Worcestershire, if you have it).

Cook this over low heat for about 20 minutes. When tofu is drained, pat dry. Then cut into rib sized pieces and fry in a little oil until golden brown. Dry off the excess oil. Place tofu on a baking pan and pour sauce on top, spreading to cover all the tofu.

Bake at 350° F for 20-30 minutes. (After you take this out of the oven, let it sit for a while so the sauce will thicken).

MACARONI CASSEROLE

Ingredients:
1 lb. macaroni noodles, cooked
1 lb. tofu cut into cubes
1 C. of corn
½ lb. mushrooms
1 small onion
2 small yellow squash
3-4 cloves of garlic
4-6 T. margarine
4-6 T. flour
2 C. soymilk
½ - ¾ C. nutritional yeast
dash of soy sauce or Bragg's to taste
½ tsp. garlic powder
¼ tsp. cayenne
Cajun seasoning to taste

Put the cooked macaroni in a large pot, and set aside. Then chop all the vegetables and garlic and cook with the cubed tofu for a few minutes. Add this to the pasta. Now melt the margarine in a large saucepan, add the flour, and whisk. Then add the soymilk and whisk until it's smooth. Add the nutritional yeast and spices and cook over low-medium heat until the sauces reach the desired thickness. Pour the sauce into the pot with the pasta-vegetables mixture and stir well. Pour it all into a BIG casserole dish and bake at 400° F for 20-30 minutes.

TURNIP STEW

Ingredients:
3-4 large turnips
1 bunch of carrots with greens attached
1 onion
4 cloves of garlic
2 tsp. fresh thyme or ½ tsp. dried
salt, pepper, cayenne, Spike seasoning to taste
2 C. vegetable stock
soymilk to thin (optional)

Peel the turnips and chop them up. Take the greens off the carrots, wash them and chop them too. Chop the carrots, onion, and garlic. Put all this in a pot with the vegetable stock and spices and cook until the turnips are soft.

Then take about half the soup and blend in a blender or food processor until it's creamy. Add this to the remaining soup in the pot stir well. Repeat this if you want a less chunky stew. Add a little soymilk to thin it if you need to. I guess you could make this recipe using potatoes instead of turnips, if you want something more substantial.

SORT OF ALFREDO

Ingredients:
fettuccine or any broad pasta, cooked
3 heads garlic
1 C. soymilk
1-2 T. olive oil for sautéing
salt and pepper to taste (about ½ tsp. each)
1 T. fresh basil
1 yellow bell pepper, sliced
1 sprig fresh rosemary, minced
1 sprig fresh thyme, minced

Preheat the oven to 375° F. Take the heads of garlic and place in a baking pan with a little bit of water. This should only cover their bottoms. Sprinkle the thyme and rosemary around in the pan. Cover the pan with foil and roast the garlic for 30-40 minutes. Then take the garlic out of the pan and let cool. When it has cooled down, squeeze all the garlic out of the peeling (this should be very easy, as roasted garlic is very soft) and put in a food processor. Add the soymilk, salt, and pepper and puree. The sauce should be creamy but not too thick. Add more soymilk, little by little, to thin it if necessary. Then, sauté the bell pepper and basil in olive oil for a few minutes. Add the garlic sauce and heat well. Serve over pasta.

INJERA

Ingredients for batter:
3 ½ C. spelt flour
1 ½ C. teff flour
4 ½ tsp. active dry yeast
5 C. warm water
2 tsp. baking powder
¼ tsp. salt

To add later:
1 tsp. baking soda
½ tsp. salt

Mix all dry ingredients together, then add warm water and stir well. Cover tightly and let sit in a relatively warm place for at least 24 hours. When it is ready it should be bubbly and smell sour. Then, add the baking soda and salt to the batter. Pour the batter into a lightly greased pan and cook like a pancake, but do not flip. You will know it is done when there are little bubbles all over the top, and the edges curl up a little.

NITER KEBBEH

Ingredients:
1 lb. unsalted margarine
1 small onion, chopped
2 cloves garlic, minced
2 tsp. fresh ginger, grated
½ tsp. tumeric
4 cardamom seeds
1 cinnamon stick
2 cloves
dash of nutmeg
¼ tsp. ground fenugreek
1 T. fresh basil, chopped

Melt the margarine, then add all other ingredients and simmer for 30-40 minutes. Strain though a mesh sieve or cheese cloth and store in an airtight container.

BERBERE

Ingredients:
2 tsp. cumin seeds
4 whole cloves
1 tsp. cardamom seeds
½ tsp. black peppercorns
¼ tsp. whole allspice
1 tsp. fennel seeds
1 tsp. fenugreek seeds
½ tsp. coriander seeds
8 small dried red chilies
½ tsp. grated fresh ginger
¼ tsp. turmeric
1 tsp. salt
2 T. Hungarian paprika
dash of ground cinnamon
dash of ground cloves

In a small frying pan on low heat, toast
cumin, whole cloves, cardamom, peppercorns,
allspice, fennel, fenugreek, and coriander for a
few minutes, stirring constantly. Remove the
pan from the heat and cool for a while. In a
spice grinder or food processor (I used a coffee
grinder), finely grind together the toasted
pieces and the chilies. Mix the remaining
ingredients. Store in an airtight container.

SHEPARD'S PIE

Ingredients:
2 lbs. potatoes
1 small onion
2 cloves garlic
2 carrots
2 turnips
1 bell pepper
1 can lentils
1 can great northern beans
1 bunch spinach
2 ears corn
2-3 T. vegetable oil plus more for sauteeing
1 T. flour
1 C. vegetable stock or soymilk
1 T. fresh thyme, minced
1 T. fresh rosemary, minced
salt and pepper to taste
2 T. nutritional yeast
½ C. soymilk
3 T. margarine

Cook the potatoes and mash them with the soymilk and margarine, and salt and pepper to taste. While the potatoes are cooking, heat some oil in a skillet and add the onion and garlic. Cook a few minutes, then add the carrots, turnips, bell peppers, lentils, northern beans, spinach and corn. Cook for a few more minutes, then set aside. (Now's the time to mash the potatoes.) In another pan, heat vegetable oil, then add one tablespoon of flour. Add to this your vegetable stock or soymilk, rosemary and thyme, and salt and pepper. Whisk until smooth and let cook on low heat until thick. Add this to the vegetable mixture, and place in a baking pan. Spread the mashed potatoes over the top and sprinkle with as much nutritional yeast as you like. Bake at 400° F for 30 minutes.

ATTAR ALLECHA

Ingredients:
½ C. onion, chopped
2 cloves garlic
1 T. oil
1 C. cooked split peas
½ tsp. turmeric
½ tsp. salt
3 tsp. hot pepper, chopped

On low heat, dry-cook the onions and garlic for a couple minutes. Add the oil and cook for another minute. Add all the other ingredients and mash well. Add water until it is a consistency you like. It should be a very thick puree.

YETAKELT WET

Ingredients:
2 C. onions
5 cloves garlic
2 T. berbere (pg. 93)
2 T. paprika
½ C. niter kebbeh (pg. 92)
1 C. green beans
1 ½ C. cabbage
2 C. carrots
2 C. potatoes
2 C. tomatoes
½ C. tomato paste
4 C. water or stock
salt and pepper to taste

Dry-cook the onions for a minute, then add the garlic, niter kebbeh, berbere, and paprika. Add all the vegetables except tomatoes and cook for 5-10 minutes. Then add all other ingredients, bring to a boil, and simmer until all vegetables are cooked. Add salt and pepper to taste.

ONION QUICHE

Ingredients:
1 package firm tofu
1 package silken tofu
½ C. flour
¾ C.soymilk
about ½ C. nutritional yeast
1 tsp. salt
¼ tsp. nutmeg
¼ tsp. turmeric
2 tsp. black pepper
2 T. fresh tarragon
2-5 cloves garlic, chopped
3-5 onions, sliced (should be about three cups after sautéing)
2 piecrusts, pre-baked for about ten minutes

Put the tofu, flour, soymilk, yeast, salt, nutmeg, and turmeric in a food processor or blender and blend until completely smooth. Set aside. Heat some oil in a large skillet, then add garlic, tarragon, black pepper and onions. Cook over medium heat until onions are caramelized, then add to the tofu mixture and stir well. Pour into pie crusts and bake at 350° F for about 40 minutes. Wait a few minutes before cutting.

ROTI

Filling Ingredients:
1 small onion, diced
4 cloves garlic, minced
4 tsp. curry powder
2 medium sized potatoes, washed, peeled, and chopped
1 carrot, grated
1 C. cooked chickpeas
½ C. chopped bell pepper
½ C. cabbage, chopped
½ C. cauliflower, chopped
1 C. water
salt to taste

Cook the onion and garlic in some oil with the curry powder. Then add the potatoes and fry for a few minutes. Add all the other vegetables and about 1 C. of water. Cover the pan and cook until the potatoes are soft and all the other vegetables are cooked. Add salt to taste.

Dough Ingredients:
1 C. flour
dash baking soda
1-4 T. soymilk
¼ tsp. salt
¼ C. vegetable oil
a handful of breadcrumbs, cornmeal, or ground chickpea flour

In a big bowl, mix flour, baking soda and salt together. Add soymilk a little at a time until you can work the dough into a ball. Divide the dough into three balls and let them rest for 10 minutes. Put the oil in a bowl so that you can get to it with your fingers. Roll out the dough on a board covered with breadcrumbs or cornmeal or ground chickpea flour. Each ball should make a circle 8 inches wide. Don't worry if it's too hard to roll out at this stage; the dough may be tough. Brush a thin layer of oil over the top surface of the circle and then scrunch it back up into a ball. Do this for all 3 balls, then let them sit for 30 minutes to rest. Then roll them out and oil them again. This time it should be easier, but they may be a little more sticky, so make sure your board and rolling pin are well floured.

Now warm a frying pan with a thick, even bottom to medium heat, no oil (there's already oil on the roti). Put one of the roti circles in and cook for about a minute. Turn it and when the hot surface cools a little, wipe it with oil. When there are some golden spots, the bread is done. Keep it between 2 plates or under a cloth to keep it soft and warm. Then put the potato curry mixture on top of the skin and fold the skin around it (like a really fat burrito). Eat this with your hands.

SIDE DISHES

COLLARD GREENS

Maybe this is self-explanatory to most people, but a lot of my friends won't eat greens 'cause they think they're too bitter. You just have to cook them until they are DONE, as in soft. Collard greens seem less bitter than mustard or turnip greens, and carrot tops cook quickly.

Ingredients:
2 small bunches or 1 large bunch of collard greens
water
1 onion, chopped
1 carrot, chopped
1 bell pepper, chopped
5-10 cloves garlic, minced
1 cube vegetable bouillon (optional)
½ tsp. liquid smoke or a tiny bit of miso (optional)

Take your greens and wash them well. Chop roughly and put in a pot. Add enough water just to cover. Then add the rest of the vegetables and bullion, if you want. Add some liquid smoke (like Stubb's) and cover and simmer the greens until they're soft. Adding the liquid smoke seems to make the greens taste more like they would if you used a meat-type seasoning. You can leave it out if that's not appealing to you.

If you don't have liquid smoke, try using miso. Just add it after the greens are cooked so you don't kill the nutrients in the miso.

ANTI PASTI

Ingredients:
2 cans fava beans
1 can chickpeas
1 bunch spinach, chopped small
1 large tomato, diced
1 jar pitted kalamata olives, chopped
2 cloves garlic, minced
juice of 1 lemon
balsamic vinegar
olive oil
cardamom

Mix together first 6 ingredients, then squeeze in lemon juice and add olive oil, balsamic vinegar and cardamom until it tastes right to you. Let this sit and marinate un-refrigerated for at least an hour before serving.

BLACK EYED PEA CAKES

Ingredients:
2 cans black eye peas
1 C. corn (fresh is better)
1 bunch green onions, chopped
1 small yellow onion, chopped
1 yellow or red bell pepper, chopped
5 cloves garlic, chopped
1 large carrot, grated
1 can coconut milk
salt, pepper, cumin, curry, thyme, cayenne, any other spices you like
cornmeal

Drain the black eye peas and place them in a big bowl and mash them with a fork or potato masher. Chop the onion, green onion, bell pepper, and garlic and add to the black eye peas along with the corn and grated carrot. Add spices, taste as you go until it seems right to you. Add coconut milk and enough cornmeal to make the mixture firm enough to hold together. You should be able to make the mixture into patties that don't fall apart. Taste the mixture for seasoning, make into cakes with your hands, and fry in canola oil until brown on both sides. Dry on paper towels.

YVETTE'S AUNT CATHY'S POTATO SALAD

Ingredients:
5 lbs. russet potatoes
2 medium Vidalia onions
1 small jar of Sweet Gherkin pickles
3 ribs celery (optional)
2-3 T. Creole or yellow mustard
½ C. vegan mayonnaise
salt, garlic powder, all purpose seasoning to taste
pickle juice, reserved

First clean and boil the potatoes whole. When they're done, split them in half and let them cool. Meanwhile, chop the rest of your vegetables, and reserve a little pickle juice for later. Peel the skins off of the cooled potatoes, cut the potatoes into chunks, and place them in a large bowl. Mix in the rest of the ingredients with your hands, adding a little pickle juice to suit your tastes. Taste as you go - start with a little and work your way up!

CARROT SALAD

Ingredients:
6-8 medium-large carrots, peeled
2 T. caraway
½-1 tsp. cayenne
salt to taste
water
2 tsp. vinegar

Slice your carrots into discs and place in a large pan with a little water, caraway, cayenne pepper, and salt. Bring to a boil, cover and simmer 30 minutes. Turn off heat and add 2 tsp. vinegar. Serve warm or at room temperature.

CRAZY HIPPIE SPRING ROLLS

A crazy hippie in Milwaukee made these for me.

Ingredients:
1 bunch red chard
1 bunch dandelion greens
1 bunch kale
1 bunch carrot greens
1 bunch green onions
about 3 carrots
½ C. grated lecithin granules
½ C. nutritional yeast
1 package spring roll wrappers
honey (this is important! if you don't eat honey, don't make this.)
juice of two lemons

Chop all the greens and green onions, and grate the carrots. Put this in a large bowl with all the other ingredients except the honey and wrappers. Prepare the spring roll wrappers and make the rolls in ordinary fashion. Then cover with honey. Dip in more honey and eat with your hands.

Ingredients:
6 bell peppers (half red, half green)
juice of 1 lemon
1 T. white/rice vinegar
1 tomato, diced
3 cloves garlic, crushed

First, roast your bell peppers. All you do is: Put said peppers on a baking sheet, turn oven to broil (about 400°) and put pan in oven. Check after about 20 minutes, and when they're black on one side, flip 'em and cook another 20 or so minutes. When both sides are black and peppers are soft, remove them from the oven, place them in a paper bag, and let them cool for a while. Then peel peppers (this should be easy), de-stem/seed, and julienne (cut into long, thin strips). Place in a bowl and add the rest of your ingredients. Let this sit at least two hours before serving.

This is one of my favorite things to eat.

WHITE BEAN BRUSCHETTA

Ingredients:
2 C. white beans
1 sprig fresh thyme
1 bay leaf
3 bulbs fennel
3 cloves garlic, minced
handful fresh basil, chopped fine
salt, pepper to taste
¼ to ½ C. water or vegetable stock
2 T. olive oil
toasted bread

Cook the white beans with the thyme and bay leaves. After the white beans are very soft, discard the thyme and bay leaf and mash the white beans well with the water or stock, and olive oil. Chop the fennel very small and add to the white beans, along with the garlic, basil, and salt, pepper and olive oil to taste.

Spread on toasted bread and serve as an appetizer. Fresh tomatoes mixed with balsamic vinegar and olive oil make a good accompaniment to this.

HUSH PUPPIES

Ingredients:
3 C. corn meal
2 tsp. baking powder
1 ½ tsp. salt
1 ½ C. soy milk
½ C. water
1 minced onion, or some minced green onions
oil for frying

Mix dry ingredients together, then add all other ingredients. Refrigerating the dough for awhile make it easier to handle. Form into 1-inch cakes and fry in oil until brown on both sides.

CREPES

Ingredients:
egg replacer for 2 eggs
1 C. soymilk
⅓ C. water
1 C. flour
2 T. sugar
1 tsp. vanilla extract
2 T. oil or melted margarine

Blend all ingredients except the oil/margarine in a blender or food processor until smooth. Put margarine on a crepe pan or non-stick pan or skillet, and use 2 or 3 tablespoons of batter for each crepe. Turn the pan when you pour in the batter so it forms a very thin layer. Flip after about 20 seconds. Serve with fresh fruit, cinnamon sugar or chocolate.

CORNMEAL MUSH

This seems to be more of a northern southern food. I ate it a lot when I was staying in North Carolina, but nobody in New Orleans seems to make it. It's a cheap breakfast food and you can make it sweet (with soymilk and syrup) or not (with Cajun seasoning and nutritional yeast).

Ingredients:
4 C. water, divided
1 C. corn meal
1 tsp. salt
a little margarine

Boil 3 C. of water. Mix the 4th cup of water with the cornmeal and salt and pour it into the boiling water. Cook awhile stirring until thick. Add some margarine and whatever seasoning you like, and serve with toast or biscuits.

QUICK PICKLED BEETS

Ingredients:
1 bunch beets
1-2 red onions, sliced
1 C. vinegar
½ C. sugar
1 T. kosher salt
1 C. water

First roast some beets: wrap them individually in foil, and bake on a cookie sheet at 400°F for 40-45 minutes. Let them cool a bit, then remove skins, tops and bottoms and slice thinly. Arrange in large jars alternating sliced beets with sliced red onions. Now boil the vinegar, sugar, kosher salt and water. Pour this over the beets, let cool, and then refrigerate. Ready to eat in 3-7 days.

VEGGIE STOCK

This can be used for making soup, sauce, gravy, to cook seitan in...

Ingredients:
10 C. water
½ C. soy sauce
1 medium size onion (white, yellow, Vidalia)
1 bell pepper
1 bunch of green onions
2 carrots
1 large handful of mushrooms
1 T. poultry or all-purpose seasoning
5-10 cloves garlic
1 T. chives
1 T. thyme
a bit of cayenne pepper

This may seem like a long list, but it's really easy to make and you can use it in a lot of different recipes. Here's what you do: Put the water and soy sauce in a large pot. Chop all the vegetables and garlic and add to pot along with herbs and spices. Bring this to a boil. Then cover and simmer for 30 minutes. When it's done you can strain out the vegetables if you want. I don't unless I'm using it to make gravy. Keep this in the freezer if you're not going to use it in a week or so.

GRAVY

Ingredients:
6 T. margarine (not oil)
½ C. nutritional yeast
½ C. flour
2 C. hot vegetable stock or hot water
1 C. soymilk
salt to taste
2 cloves garlic, crushed
½ tsp. onion powder
a few cloves of garlic, chopped

Melt the margarine in a large pan. Add the garlic and spices,
then add the flour and stir until it clumps together. Add the
stock or water and stir (a whisk works best) until smooth.
Add the nutritional yeast and soymilk and mix until gravy is
creamy. Turn the heat down and stir until gravy reaches the
desired thickness. This will keep in the fridge for about a week.

MUSHROOM GRAVY

by Yoni

A reasonable approximation of how I make mushroom gravy.
1. The essentials: Mushrooms, margarine, flour, onions, black
pepper, water

2: Highly recommended: Some celery, a bit of nutritional yeast,
salt, and soy sauce

3. Also kinda nice: A clove or two of garlic, other spices you like,
maybe some fake meat(?)

4. "But how?" you ask...

Chop up the mushrooms and onions (celery, garlic...) into your
preferred size and sauté them in margarine with lots of black
pepper (and other spices) in a really big pan over medium heat
for quite some time (all these prepositions are making you a better cook right now. I swear.)

Have the flour and water on hand. When the mushrooms are soft, pour in some water, followed a few moments later by some pinches of flour and vigorous stirring with a whisk or fork. At this point I just repeat the water/flour/stir steps 'til I've arrived at what seems like the appropriate thickness and amount and/or I've grown tired of it, all the while obsessively adding tiny amounts of salt to try and get it just right.

5. "But wait! How much?"

Oh, figure it out yourself, you big baby.... Really, I never pay much attention. Though the other day I used a small onion and maybe 4 mushrooms and they flavored up enough gravy for 4 people. So maybe extrapolate from there. By volume I'd recommend a bit more mushroom than onion and significantly less celery than either.

On that note, some of y'all are probably hollering about how I should've said lots of garlic and a ton of nutritional yeast. To which I reply: SHUT UP! I mean, you go do whatever you want, but remember it's a MUSHROOM gravy (un-)recipe; and mushrooms, onion and celery got lots of flavor. I love garlic as much as you, got the garlic tattoo to prove it, but we should all remember that it's possible to make good and even amazing food without garlic. And nutritional yeast gravy is a whole 'nother recipe.

6. The End

Thanks for reading, sorry that took so long. I talk like this too.

DRES$ING

Ingredients:
1 lb. brown sugar
⅛ C. kosher salt
1 T. paprika
⅛ C. black pepper
1 T. fresh thyme
4 minced garlic cloves
zest from two lemons

Mix all ingredients together and place on baking sheet

BBQ SAUCE

overnight, so sugar dries out. Then grind into powder in a food processor. That's it. Use on tofu, seitan, vegetables, etc.

Sautee 1 chopped onion and 1 clove of chopped garlic in some oil.

When the onions are translucent add:

Simmer sauce on low heat for 30 minutes. Blend in a blender or in a food processor.

2 T. Worcestershire sauce (make sure it doesn't have anchovies!)
1 T. soy sauce
1 C. water
1 minced jalapeño
2 T. vinegar
2 T. brown sugar
1 C. tomato sauce
1 tsp. Creole mustard
½ tsp. of salt
¼ tsp. cinnamon
½ tsp. cumin
¼ tsp. ginger

LEMON DIJON

Ingredients:
¾ C. Dijon mustard
juice of 3 lemons
¾ C. vinegar
4 T. honey or maple syrup
2 C. oil
1 ½ tsp. salt

In a large bowl, combine all ingredients except oil. Then slowly
whisk in oil while pouring it in a steady stream to emulsify.

CRANBERRY DRESSING

Ingredients:
4 minced shallots
¾ C. Dijon mustard
2 cans cranberries (or cranberry sauce)
8 oz. cranberry juice
1 ¼ C. vinegar (rice vinegar is good)
2 C. olive oil
salt and pepper to taste

Blend all ingredients except oil in blender. Then put this mixture
into a bowl and whisk oil in slowly. That's all.

STRAWBERRY DRESSING

Ingredients:
2 packages frozen strawberries
lots of balsamic vinegar
2-3 T. Dijon mustard
1 clove garlic, minced
1 shallot, minced
salt and pepper to taste
about 2 C. olive or vegetable oil

Put the frozen strawberries in a pot. Pour enough balsamic vinegar over
to cover (a whole lot) and cook on medium heat, stirring occasionally,
until it's reduced to a syrupy liquid. Put this reduction in a blender with
the mustard, garlic, shallot, salt and pepper.

With blender on, slowly add oil olive or vegetable oil. Taste as you go-
you'll probably need about 2 C. of oil. This makes a LOT of dressing but
it will last for weeks.

DESSERTS

PEACH TURNOVERS

Ingredients:
1 C. vegetable shortening (Crisco)
⅔ C. boiling water
½ tsp. salt
1 tsp. baking powder
3 C. flour
3-4 large ripe peaches, diced
1 tsp. vanilla
sugar

Put the shortening in a bowl and pour the boiling water over it. Stir until the shortening is dissolved. Add the salt and baking powder, stir well, and then add the flour. Knead into a ball and refrigerate the dough for at least an hour.

When dough is ready, toss the peaches with a little vanilla. Roll the dough out and cut into 4-inch circles. Put about 1 T. of peaches in the center of each circle, and sprinkle with sugar. Then wet the edges of the circle and pinch shut. Use the tines of a fork to press along the edges. Place the turnovers on a greased and floured baking sheet, brush them with water or soymilk and sprinkle sugar on top. Bake at 425° F for 20 minutes. This makes about 12 turnovers.

(I adapted this from a recipe in the *Fannie Farmer Cookbook*).

RED VELVET CAKE

Ingredients:
½ C. margarine
1 ½ C. sugar
egg replacer for 2 eggs
1 tsp. vanilla
1 cup soymilk mixed with 1 T. vinegar
1 small bottle red food coloring
⅓ C. cocoa
2 C. flour
1 tsp. salt
1 ½ tsp. baking powder

Cream together the sugar and margarine, then add egg replacer and vanilla and mix well. Stir together the soy milk/vinegar mixture with food coloring. Then in another bowl combine the dry ingredients. Add the dry ingredients to margarine mixture alternately with soymilk mixture, mixing well. Pour into a greased and floured pan and bake at 350° F for 30-35 minutes. Frost however you like.

DOUGHNUTS

This is an incredibly time and labor-intensive recipe.

Ingredients:

STEP 1:
a little flour
½ tsp. active dry yeast
1 C. warm water
1 C. flour

STEP 2:
1 stick margarine
2 T. vegetable shortening
⅔ C. sugar
2 tsp. vanilla extract
egg replacer for 3 eggs
3 ½ C. flour
and enough oil to fry with

What to do:

STEP 1: Sprinkle a tiny bit of flour and the active dry yeast over warm water. Let this sit for about 5 minutes, or until yeast is dissolved. Then add flour, cover tightly and let sit for 45 minutes.

STEP 2: In another bowl, mix together margarine, shortening, and sugar. Add to this the and egg replacer (Ener-G definitely works best for this) and stir well. Add this to the yeast mixture along with the 3 ½ C. flour. Mix the dough until it starts to pull away from the sides of the bowl. It will be very sticky.

Place the dough in a well-oiled bowl, cover well and let rise for an hour or two in a warm place. Then put the dough in a plastic bag and refrigerate overnight. It will be ready to use the next day.

Just make the dough into whatever shapes you please and fry in oil. They're best covered with powdered sugar and eaten with coffee while they're still warm.

I never said making good doughnuts was easy!

ESPRESSO CAKE

Ingredients:
4 tsp. instant espresso
3 T. boiling water
⅓ C. soymilk
1 ½ C. flour
½ tsp. baking soda
½ tsp. baking powder
¼ tsp. salt
6 T. margarine
¾ C. of sugar
2 tsp. vanilla
egg replacer for 2 eggs

Cream the margarine with the sugar and vanilla. Dissolve the espresso in the boiling water and add to the margarine mixture, along with the egg replacer and soymilk. Then mix together the flour, baking soda, baking powder and salt and fold this into the wet ingredients. Beat only until the batter is smooth and free of any lumps. Bake in a greased floured pan at 350° F for 20-25 minutes.

I usually just glaze this cake with a ganache made by melting chocolate chips with a little soymilk or a shot of espresso, and some vanilla.

CHOCOLATE PEPPERMINT MOUSSE

Ingredients:
¾ C. sugar
½ C. water
2 C. chocolate chips
2 packages silken tofu
1 ½ C. soymilk
1 tsp. vanilla
1 tsp. mint extract
½ tsp. of salt
2 T. vegetable oil

Put the water, sugar, and tofu in a blender and blend on high until smooth. Then melt the chocolate chips with the soymilk and add this and all the other ingredients to the blender. Blend until all is smooth and freeze in an airtight container, stirring every few hours until it's frozen. Or, if you're lucky enough to have an ice-cream maker, freeze it that way.

YVETTE BAGUETTES BOYCLOTS

(a measurement-free recipe!)

Ingredients:
rolled oats
margarine
honey or pure maple syrup
peanut butter
nuts, chopped (Yvette likes almonds)
brown sugar
chocolate chips

Melt margarine in a skillet. Add brown sugar. Stir constantly so it doesn't burn. Add the honey or maple syrup. Stir and add chocolate chips and peanut butter. Stir some more until chocolate chips are melted and you have an insanely sweet brown gloppy mess in aforementioned skillet. Combine the nuts with the oats. Remove the sweet goo from the stove and pour into the nuts/oats. Stick your hands in and mix it up. Form into balls. Grease a pan, put the balls in and simply broil for 10 minutes (your oven will have a broil setting). Yo, you got yourself some boyclots. They fall apart if you don't give them time to cool off before eating...

P.S.—You know they're right if they look vaguely like cat puke.

WHEAT FREE LEMON COOKIES

Ingredients:
2 sticks margarine
1 C. sugar
egg replacer for 2 eggs
1 tsp. vanilla
1-2 tsp. lemon flavoring
2 ½ C. spelt flour

Cream together the margarine and sugar. Then add egg replacer, vanilla and lemon flavoring and stir. Add the flour, stir well, and refrigerate the dough for at least an hour. Then, roll the dough into balls, and bake at 375° F for about 8 minutes.

VIRGINIA SINGLETON McGHEE'S FRUIT COOKIES

(veganized version)

Ingredients:
2 lbs. pitted dates
½ lb. candied cherries
½ lb. candied pineapples
½ lb. shelled blanched almonds
½ lb. pecans
2 ½ C. sifted flour
1 tsp. baking soda
1 tsp. salt
1 tsp. cinnamon
1 ½ C. sugar
egg replacer for 2 eggs
1 C. margarine

Cut dates and fruit into small chunks. Toast almonds until golden (about 10 minutes). Chop pecans. Sift flour, baking soda, salt and cinnamon together. Preheat oven to 375° F.

Cream margarine and sugar together, then add egg replacer and beat until smooth. Then add in flour mixture and all fruit and nuts. Drop by heaping teaspoonfuls onto a baking sheet. Bake for 10 minutes. Makes about 100 cookies.

MINT JULEP SORBET

Ingredients:
2 C. fresh mint
2 C. sugar
2 C. water
pinch of salt
2 tsp. lemon juice
¼ C. whiskey

Combine all ingredients in a large pot, bring to a boil, and remove from heat. Let sit for 2 hours then strain and freeze. If you have an ice cream machine, use it. If not, stir the sorbet every once in a while.

ALMOST PAULA DEEN'S BLUEBERRY BUCKLE

Ingredients:
1 C. sugar
1 stick salted margarine
1 tsp. vanilla extract
¼ C. lemon soy yogurt
dash of nutmeg
2 C. flour
2 tsp. baking powder
zest of 1 lemon
½ C. soymilk
1 C. blueberries

Topping:
¼ C. cold margarine
½ C. brown sugar
½ C. flour
2 tsp. cinnamon

In a bowl, cream together well the sugar and margarine. Then add the vanilla, yogurt, and nutmeg. Separately, combine the flour, baking powder, and lemon zest. Add this to margarine mixture along with the soymilk—start with ½ cup and add more, little by little, if you need. Fold in the blueberries. Pour into greased and floured pan. Separately, combine the crumb topping ingredients and top your batter. Bake at 350° F for about 30 minutes.

AMALGAMATION CAKE

Aka "Tennessee Jam Cake"

Ingredients:
1 C. sugar
¾ C. vegan margarine (Earth Balance is good)
1 C. strawberry jam
1 tsp. vanilla
½ C. plain soy yogurt
1 ½ tsp. Ener-G egg replacer mixed with 2 T. water
2 C. flour
1 ½ tsp. baking soda
½ tsp. nutmeg
½ tsp. allspice
½ tsp. cinnamon
½ tsp. cloves
½ C. soy milk mixed with 1 tsp. vinegar to make soy buttermilk

Cream together sugar and margarine. Add the strawberry jam, vanilla, yogurt, and egg replacer/water mixture. Stir well. In another bowl, combine flour, baking soda, and your 4 spices. Add this to sugar mixture alternately with soy buttermilk and stir well. Pour into greased and floured 9" pans, bake at 350° F for 30 minutes.

I usually frost this with a coconut-pecan frosting, which is just caramelized sugar and margarine mixed with shredded coconut, chopped pecans, and powdered sugar. Hey, guess okay? It's fun!

MING TSAI'S GINGERBREAD

Ingredients:
⅔ C. cake flour
⅔ C. all purpose flour
1 tsp. baking soda
¼ tsp. cinnamon
⅓ tsp. cloves
⅛ tsp. black pepper
½ C. sugar
egg replacer for 1 egg
½ C. canola oil
½ C. molasses
¼ C. candied ginger
½ C. water

Sift together dry ingredients. Add everything else, stir just until combined and not lumpy (well, except for the ginger). Bake at 300° F for 20-30 minutes. Serve with coffee or espresso.

CHOCOLATE KAHULA CAKE

Ingredients:
(6) 1 oz. squares of bittersweet chocolate
1 C. sugar
2 T. vanilla
1 ½ sticks margarine
egg replacer for 3 eggs
1 T. baking powder
½ tsp. salt
½ C. Kahlua mixed with ½ cup water
2 ½ C. flour

Glaze:
¼ C. Kahlua
½-1 C. powdered sugar

Melt the chocolate with the margarine and vanilla. Add the sugar and stir until smooth, then add your egg replacer. Mix together the flour, salt, and baking powder and add the chocolate mixture alternately with Kahlua-water mixture. Pour into a well-greased and floured pan and bake at 350° F until a toothpick inserted into the cake comes out clean. Blend the Kahlua and powdered sugar, glaze the cake, and dust with cinnamon.

BLUEBERRY OR CHOCOLATE PEANUT BUTTER BANANA BREAD

Ingredients:
3-4 mashed bananas
½ C. sugar
½ C. oil or margarine
2 T. vanilla
1 tsp. cinnamon
1 ½-2 cups flour
½ tsp. salt
2 tsp. baking powder
¼ tsp. baking soda
1 container blueberries OR
1 C. chocolate chips and 2 T. peanut butter
¼ C. soymilk

Mix the bananas with the sugar, oil, vanilla, and cinnamon. (Add the peanut butter too, if you're making the chocolate chip version).
Mix the dry ingredients together and add to the wet ingredients. Now add chocolate chips or blueberries.
If the batter looks too thick, add some soymilk; if it's too thin add some more flour. Pour the batter into a greased and floured pan and bake at 375° F for 30-40 minutes.

CARMEL FUDGE FROSTING

Ingredients:
1 C. brown sugar
¼ C. margarine
1 tsp. vanilla extract
2-3 tsp. water
2 oz. unsweetened chocolate

In a sauce pan, combine brown sugar, margarine, vanilla and water. Cook until the sugar is caramelized, then add unsweetened chocolate. Cook until soft-ball stage*, adding a little water if necessary. Spread on cake immediately, as it will harden upon standing.

*Test for soft-ball stage by dropping a bit into cold water. It should form a ball that quickly dissolves. If the ball stays solid, you've cooked it too long.

SWEET POTATO PUDDING

Ingredients:
¼ C. margarine
½ C. sugar
¼ C. brown sugar
egg replacer for 2 eggs (I use 1/2 cup of applesauce mixed with 2-3 spoons of baking powder)
1 tsp. cinnamon
¼ tsp. nutmeg
¼ tsp. cloves
1 T. vanilla
dash of salt
2 ½ C. shredded sweet potatoes (uncooked)
1 ½ C. soymilk or soy creamer

Mix together the sugar, margarine, and brown sugar in a big bowl. Add the egg replacer, spices, and salt and stir.

Then add the sweet potatoes and soymilk (or cream) and stir well. Pour this into a greased casserole dish and bake at 400° F for about an hour.

Sauce for pudding:

Ingredients:
½ C. brown sugar
½ C. margarine
1 tsp. vanilla
¼ C. whiskey

Stir all this together in a small saucepan over low-medium heat. bring to a boil, then add ½ C. of water and stir well. You can add 1 T. cornstarch to thicken, if you want. You can also add more whiskey if you want it stronger.

Ingredients:
2 C. cooked or canned pumpkin
2 T. soymilk
4 T. arrowroot mixed with 1/2 cup of water
OR
½ C. applesauce mixed with 2 T. baking powder
OR
any other egg substitute (for 2 eggs)
2 T. oil
1 C. flour
3 T. sugar
1 tsp. baking powder
½ tsp. salt
½ tsp. cinnamon
a bit of nutmeg

In a large bowl mash up the pumpkin. Then add the soymilk, egg substitute, and oil. Mix until smooth. Combine the flour, sugar, baking powder, salt, cinnamon, and nutmeg in another bowl. Add this to the pumpkin mixture and stir well. If the batter looks too thick you can add some more flour. Drop the batter by spoonfuls into hot oil and deep fry until browned on both sides. Drain off excess oil with paper towels and sprinkle with powdered sugar.

PARTY IN YOUR MOUTH CAKE

Ingredients:
2 C. sugar
1 C. margarine
2 T. vanilla
½ C. applesauce mixed with 2 T. baking powder
2 ½ -3 C. flour
3 tsp. baking powder
1 tsp. salt
1 ½ C. soy milk
1 container of raspberries
1 container of strawberries
1 orange
1 C. chocolate chips

Cream the margarine and sugar together, then add the vanilla and applesauce-baking powder mixture.

Mix together the flour, baking powder, and salt, and add to the sugar mixture alternately with soymilk until everything's all mixed together. Then add the container of raspberries and stir well. Pour the batter into 2 greased and floured pans of equal size (because it's going to be a 2 layer cake) and bake at 350° F for about 30-40 minutes. While the cake is baking, slice some strawberries. Toss them in a bowl with some vanilla, sugar and the juice from the orange, and set this aside.

When the cake is done (cooled too), place one layer on a plate or the cake dish. Take the strawberries and spread on top. Now carefully add the top layer. Melt the chocolate chips with some margarine and water and cook over low heat until it thickens. Swirl the chocolate sauce over the cake in fancy (or not so fancy) designs, and decorate with strawberry slices along the cakes edges.